LOOK AT MORE

A PROVEN APPROACH TO INNOVATION, GROWTH, AND CHANGE

ANDY STEFANOVICH

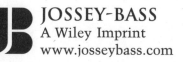

JOSSEY-BASS
A Wiley Imprint
www.josseybass.com

Published by Jossey-Bass
A Wiley Imprint
989 Market Street, San Francisco, CA 94103-1741—www.josseybass.com

Readers should be aware that Internet Web sites offered as citations and/or sources for further information may have changed or disappeared between the time this was written and when it is read.

Jossey-Bass books and products are available through most bookstores. To contact Jossey-Bass directly call our Customer Care Department within the U.S. at 800-956-7739, outside the U.S. at 317-572-3986, or fax 317-572-4002.

Jossey-Bass also publishes its books in a variety of electronic formats. Some content that appears in print may not be available in electronic books.

Library of Congress Cataloging-in-Publication Data

Stefanovich, Andy.
    Look at more : a proven approach to innovation, growth, and change / Andy Stefanovich.
      p. cm.
    Includes bibliographical references and index.
  ISBN 978-0-470-94977-1 (hardback); ISBN 978-1-118-01959-7 (ebk);
  ISBN 978-1-118-01960-3 (ebk); ISBN 978-1-118-01961-0 (ebk)
  1.   Creative ability in business. 2.   Creative thinking. 3.   New products.
  4.   Technological innovations. 5.   Organizational change. I. Title.
  HD53.S7366 2011
  658.4′063-dc22

                         2010051340

CONTENTS

Introduction 1

Chapter 1 Mood 19

Chapter 2 Mindset 47

Chapter 3 Mechanisms 91

Chapter 4 Measurement 129

Chapter 5 Momentum 143

Chapter 6 Full Circle: The Sixth M 167

Appendix: The Scientific Stuff 171
Notes 181
Acknowledgments 187
About the Author 191
Index 193

LOOK AT MORE

INTRODUCTION

Hi. The book you're holding in your hands is not your ordinary volume on innovation. It's not another book on brainstorming or Six Sigma, and it's not about methodology or models or theory. Don't get me wrong—I have nothing against most of those things. In fact, I've used a lot of them in my professional life. But for the most part, these approaches have taken the humanity out of innovation and made it dry and mechanical or—even worse—complex and confusing. Companies of every size and in every sector have been focusing so hard and so long on innovation that in some cases, the whole process has ground to a halt. They simply can't get out of their own way.

After twenty years of helping some of the biggest companies in the world become more innovative, I can tell you that the most effective way to unleash innovation is through *inspiration*. Inspiration fuels creativity, and creative thinkers innovate. That's it. The problem with most fancy innovation theories, methodologies, models, and all the rest is that they just don't inspire.

So how *do* we inspire people? Well, we have to learn to think differently and encourage others to do the same. Unfortunately, for most of us, that's not a transition that happens all by itself. Becoming an inspired individual is a rigorous discipline that requires practice. It's also an *approach* to innovation that Play, the company I founded twenty years ago, brought to clients—the same approach I'll be showing you in this book. The discipline of inspiration is so important and valuable for business, in fact, that we sold the company to Prophet, a global brand and marketing consultancy, in 2009 so that we could expand the reach of our process into the strategy of more leading companies around the world.

We call that process LAMSTAIH, which stands for *Look at More Stuff; Think About It Harder*. LAMSTAIH (pronounced "lamb's tie") is written in five-foot-high letters in my office, and it has become part of the daily vocabulary of some of the largest corporations in the world (who hire us to help them acquire the practical skills, leadership behavior, and cultural mindset to create ideas and drive innovation). As you're about to learn, LAMSTAIH is less complicated, easier to learn, and a lot more effective (and by that I mean more likely to inspire) than the other approaches to innovation that you may have come across. In fact, learning to think differently just takes common sense.

Because we're going to be spending quite a bit of time together, there's something about me that you should know right now. I love stories. I love listening to them, and I love telling them. I believe that when asking a question, the goal should be a story, not an answer. And, because every organization's situation is unique, there *are* no right answers. So instead of giving answers, I'm going to spend most of this book telling you stories. Some of them are from my own life or business experience. Some were told to me by friends and colleagues. And some, I'll admit, I've clipped out of magazines and newspapers for no other reason than that they nicely illustrate a point. Some of these stories will resonate with you personally or professionally, and others won't. Some you'll want to share. Others may annoy you, and still others will seem totally random. In fact, I sometimes rely on what I call "purposeful disruptions," which are extremely valuable for driving home some important messages.

My goal here is to give you both quantity and variety in the information you'll read in this book. I have faith that you'll be able to find the message in the stories, apply it to your own situation, and reach your own conclusions. After all, what kind of hypocrite would I be if in the process of trying to teach you to think differently I insisted that you stick to a rigid formula?

You can think of reading this book as kind of like going to a museum. Not every exhibit—or individual piece within the exhibit—will blow your mind. Chances are, though, that *something* in the museum will move you. Having the right curator to guide you through the exhibits and explain certain works can go a long way toward making your visit relevant and inspiring—that's the role I'll be playing as we move through the book.

By the time you finish this book, I know you'll have found at least a handful of ideas that will make you think differently about the topics of innovation and creativity that will help you become a more inspired and inspiring individual. If you haven't, I will have failed. But in more than twenty years of using this approach with companies and executives around the world, it's been a great success. I've seen over and over how two or three thoughts or ideas can completely transform a company and all the individuals who work there. The same thing *will* happen with you and your organization.

Let me start with a story about a guy named Phillip McCrory, who created a transformational innovation while sitting at home on his day off, while drinking coffee and watching television.

It was the last week of March 1989, and like so many others, McCrory was glued to CNN taking in the devastation wrought by the nearly eleven million gallons of oil that had spilled from the Exxon *Valdez* tanker into Alaska's Prince William Sound. McCrory, who at the time was a hairdresser in Madison, Alabama, watched a rescue worker struggle to clean the sticky mess off the fur of a traumatized otter. The oil seemed fused to the animal's coat. Then the inspiration hit McCrory: "If fur can trap and hold spilled oil, why shouldn't human hair work equally as well?"[1]

Where most people saw only tragedy, McCrory saw a solution. Could the millions of pounds of hair put in landfills each year be a new solution to horrific environmental disasters? Minutes later, McCrory was in the car, heading to his salon.

Already the holder of several patents for hair styling products, McCrory was ready to start experimenting. He took a pair of his wife's pantyhose and stuffed them with five pounds of clippings from the salon floor. He tied the feet of the hose together to form a ring with a slip knot and placed it into his son's plastic swimming pool, which he filled to the brim with water. He then poured used motor oil into the center of the ring, pulled the slip knot to make the ring smaller, and watched with excitement as all the oil attached itself to the hair. Within just a few minutes, he couldn't see a trace of oil in the water at all.

It turns out that human hair doesn't absorb oil: it *ad*sorbs it—oil clings to the hair rather than soaking into it. As a result, the hair can be wrung out and used again and again. The oil itself can be recovered and reused, too.

Recognizing the opportunity, McCrory set out for NASA's Marshall Space Flight Center in nearby Huntsville, where scientists at the Technology Transfer Center took great interest. Initial tests showed that McCrory's method could clear a gallon of oil in less than two minutes for about $2. Prevailing solutions at that time were far more complicated, took longer, and cost around $10 for every gallon of oil cleared.

Years later, McCrory received a patent and started his own company. The ripple effects of his innovation are still spreading around the world. In 2006, the Philippine government collected one hundred thousand garbage bags of hair, which they used to clean up fifty-three thousand gallons of oil that had spilled off the nation's coast. All kinds of people—including schoolchildren and prison inmates—contributed. And the concept continues to evolve. One company transforms a single pound of hair (roughly the daily amount collected at the average salon) into a one-foot-square, half-inch-thick mat that can absorb up to a quart of oil and be reused one hundred times. In 2007, these mats were used to clean up spills in San Francisco, and McCrory's discovery was mobilized again during the 2010 oil leak in the Gulf of Mexico.

Okay, you might be thinking, big deal—so some hairdresser came up with a clever way of soaking up oil. It *is* a big deal, and for multiple reasons. First, this story is a perfect example of inspiration in action, of how a single moment of inspiration can turn into an innovation that changes the world. But even more important, it shows that you won't find new solutions if you keep looking at the same things in the same ways. And that's how most people spend the majority of their time: talking to the same experts, reading the same trade mags, poring over the same deck of market data, looking at the same

Web sites, eating lunch at the same place, driving home the same way, asking the same questions, giving the same answers, using the same tools, applying the same measures for success, and so on.

It's a good thing those scientists at NASA's Technology Transfer Center were willing to step outside their usual routines and talk with McCrory. As unlikely as it might seem for an organization involved in cleaning up oil spills to take a meeting with an Alabama hairdresser, in retrospect, it makes perfect sense. Why wouldn't scientists who clean the oil off of furry creatures want to hear the ideas of someone who deals with oily hair every day? How would you like to have someone like McCrory on your team? To find the unexpected, you have to be open to it—wherever and whenever it appears.

Focus on Input Instead of Output

You can't wander through a corporate headquarters these days without bumping into the chief innovation officer, who's just come from a meeting with her innovation council in the recently completed, state-of-the-art innovation room, where they sat frowning at the results of their efforts to create a "culture of innovation" that could live up to their number one corporate value: innovation. Why don't they have that culture? Why can't these companies get the kind of inspiration that Phillip McCrory had?

The answer is simple, but counterintuitive: most companies look for innovation in the wrong places, by focusing on the intended *output* instead of the *input*. True innovation—and by that I mean the kind that changes you, your team, your organization, and the world—comes from a completely new kind of thinking. And that, of course, is what LAMSTAIH—looking at more stuff and thinking about it harder—is all about. As we progress through the book, you're going to learn what kind of stuff we're supposed to be looking at and what it means to "think about it harder."

Unfortunately, at most companies, old habits (including looking in the wrong places) are hard to break. No matter how much they talk about the importance of inspiration, when these organizations truly set aside time to create, the everyday pressures and routines of modern business push them back into their old ways. I've seen it happen a thousand times: people walk out of an energetic, creative session where inspiration flowed freely and their team generated a ton of great ideas. But by the time they get back to their desks, their heads are down and they're back to doing whatever they were doing before. By the next day, it's as if they were never inspired at all.

One problem is that the word *innovation* is, in many ways, an obstacle to itself. It gets bandied around so much these days that it's become almost meaningless. A bigger issue, however, is that most organizations aren't set up to encourage employees to seek inspiration. In fact, in surveying thousands of business leaders with our partner, Kim Jaussi of Binghamton University, we found that only 27 percent said they were inspired by their own supervisors; that leaves more than *two-thirds* of our respondents lacking inspiration from their leaders.[2] Most companies don't measure or reward inspiration and creativity. Instead, employees are motivated to work quickly and efficiently, to check off one task and then move on to the next. In other words, they aren't paid to think—at least not creatively.

The solution? You have to learn to be comfortable looking for inspiration in the opposite direction of the places you normally look. I know that for a lot of companies, doing a 180 from the current innovation process is going against the laws of physics. But it can be done. Sustainable innovation begins with inspired employees. So your first step is to take a deep breath and stop worrying about the bottom line so much. Instead, you're going to start paying attention to your responsibility for inspiring every individual within your organization. That means making some big changes—to your expectations, to the methods you use to measure success, and to the ways you reward outstanding performance. It also means making a concerted effort to seek out inspiration for new business ideas, usually in places you've never thought of before.

Learning to look for inspiration in everything you do and everywhere you go is critical to the process of building creative thinking skills. Thinking differently is a learned skill, one you'll have to practice the rest of your life. Only rigid thinkers believe they have mastered creativity. Most great musicians and athletes spend a lot more time practicing than they do performing or competing with other teams—that's how they hone their skills and discipline. Running through a series of drills or playing scales for hours on end are demanding and sometimes boring exercises. But when the musician finally takes the stage or the athlete steps onto the field, the time and energy they put into their practice pays off.

We understand that superb musical or athletic performance demands extensive practice, so why don't we treat the discipline of seeking out inspiration for new ideas in businesses the same way? Sure, there are rare individuals, like Phillip McCrory, whose inspiration seems to come out of nowhere. In most cases, though, inspiration happens—to paraphrase the old saying—when preparation meets opportunity. In other words, it's all about training yourself to think differently and creatively so that when the opportunity arises, you'll know what you need to do.

That's the kind of thinking you're about to learn.

Don't Wait for a Stroke of Brilliance

We have a tendency to think of inspiration as the proverbial lightning strike—one of those things that just happens, that you can't engineer. But that's a pretty limited characterization. There are actually three different ways that we get inspired: by delight, by design, and on demand. Let's take a closer look:

- **Inspiration by delight.** These are the purely serendipitous moments we've all had at one time or another. You're suddenly moved by a scene on the street, the beauty of nature, or the shockingly wise words of a child. You didn't plan for it, but you were in the right place at the right time. Understanding the physiological and mental dynamics at play during moments of pure surprise and delight is critical to channeling inspiration toward a specific objective.

- **Inspiration by design.** This is when you intentionally put yourself in a situation where there's a higher likelihood of getting inspired, such as going to see an art show or taking a class with a brilliant teacher. Unfortunately, we often limit ourselves to finding inspiration from relatively few sources—museums, theaters, classrooms, and so on. But if you keep working at it, you can expand your capacity for finding inspiration in other, less obvious places. The inspiration you need for your business isn't necessarily going to be where you might commonly look. And although you can't predict the outcome of inspiration by design, you can predict the cost of *not* seeking out inspiration: your thinking will grow stale, and you'll drastically limit the possibilities before you.

- **Inspiration on demand.** Like it or not, in our daily business lives we sometimes need inspiration on a moment's notice, but don't have the time, resources, or permission to hunt for it. This is like on-demand TV: the entertainment industry built a model around how people want to watch TV, archiving it because we demand to view it on our own terms.

Focusing on each kind of inspiration makes all three of them a stronger influence in your creative process. For example, the more you seek out inspiration by design and the more you practice inspiration on demand, the more likely you are to be fully aware when you're inspired by delight. You'll also be better able to apply those elegant moments of inspiration to your own life and work.

Some people might argue that you can't create serendipity, but over the last two decades, I've learned that you can indeed push yourself and your team to unforeseen insights and meaning with a combination of openness and a little faith. So even though I can't teach you how to get lightning to strike where and when you want it, I will show you a number of techniques and perspectives for whipping up a storm of inspiration, creativity, and innovation. Once you experience the power to look at more stuff and think about it harder, you'll be able to give others a taste of this process and create an army of empowered and inspired individuals who will help your organization find new avenues for growth.

Become the Curator of Inspiration

Whenever I travel somewhere with colleagues, we build in a bit of time for finding inspiration. In 2003, Courtney Ferrell and I were in Chicago finishing up some work with Crate & Barrel, and in the second half of the day before our flight back to Richmond, we headed down to the Museum of Contemporary Art.

We bought our tickets and joined hundreds of others in the quiet contemplation of the museum's paintings, sculpture, and multimedia installations. And, of course, we also studied our fellow museum goers—their clothes, their mannerisms, their conversations and questions, and the way they scrunched their faces while trying to decide what some piece was all about.

As we slowly shuffled along a wall of paintings, in line with a dozen other people, Courtney stopped and wrote "museum mentality" on a Think Card—a three-and-a-half-inch square, red card we use to record moments of inspiration. (Inspiration can evaporate in a moment, so we always carry these cards to record inspired ideas as they occur. I've recorded over thirty thousand Think Cards so far, and I'll share some of them with you throughout this book.) Here's the inspiration that Courtney recorded on her card that day:

Why *do* we give ourselves permission to be inspired inside the museum? Is it just because we've paid to get in, so we can trust the information fed to us by the museum's expert curators? I think that when we buy a ticket to an event or travel somewhere we've never been before, we instinctively expect that kind of return on our investment. But we don't have that same expectation of our day-to-day activities. Which is why it's harder to feel inspired by familiar people, events, or surroundings.

Museum Mentality

Isn't it amazing? We give ourselves permission to find inspiration in a museum because we expect it. We pay to get in and we trust someone else to give two-sentence explanations of everything on the walls. But then we walk out the door and we put on our blinders again. We leave the experience and the wonder behind. How can we have a museum mentality everywhere in our lives? At home? At work? On a random street corner?

THINK

If you're like me, you probably spend the majority of your waking hours (and sometimes your dreams) trying to deliver value for yourself, your team, and your organization. So why not take control of the experience of everyday life and become a curator of inspiration for yourself and others?

Twenty years ago, I decided that I wanted to change the world. I needed to find the "Bigger Big," a way to make a difference on a personal and professional level that would have an impact far beyond my immediate circle. I firmly believe that all of us find our own way to the Bigger Big by embracing the discipline of inspiration and incorporating it into our daily lives. The majority of this book is about bringing inspiration to business, because business in its many forms touches everyone—employees and their families, customers and suppliers, shareholders and governments, the rich and the poor. The impact of inspiration goes on and on, and finding the Bigger Big will add a note of happiness to your life. Really.

As a leader and adviser, I don't see myself as a manager, motivator, or ultimate problem solver. I see myself as a curator. I discover and edit the excellence of the world and bring the best new perspectives and insights to inspire other people so that they can deliver great innovations. That's how I view my role every day. It's why I put my feet on the ground each morning. And it is now my formal position at Prophet: chief curator and provocateur.

I think I'd always considered myself a curator of sorts, but I didn't fully grasp the idea until I met Paola Antonelli, the senior curator of architecture and design at the Museum of Modern Art in New York City. We found that we had a surprisingly similar view of our roles and responsibilities. Over the course of several conversations, Antonelli explained to me her ideas about the three kinds of curators:

- The traditional definition—what the French call conservateurs. These curators are the keepers of objects, the ones charged with preserving and cataloging, storing and protecting. Their role is to make sure that people hundreds of years in the future can benefit from an experience with an object. That's probably where a lot of minds go when they first think of curators. You can imagine a weathered academic walking through row after row of dusty crates in a giant warehouse, each filled with precious artifacts from antiquity. He knows where everything is, and he knows its history, but in many ways, his job is to keep things hidden and safe until the time is right to reveal them. But that's only one kind of curator.

- Zeitgeist curators are people with acute intuition who listen to the world and find just the right materials to capture for an audience the essence of the times. They aren't thinking too far into the future, predicting what the world will need. Instead, they capture the spirit of today and connect it to the near tomorrow.

- Hunter-gatherer curators constantly search the world for the most compelling and interesting things that should be shared.

Antonelli (who sees herself as a hunter-gatherer with a touch of the zeitgeist) is on a never-ending mission to find things that catch her attention. She might not immediately know how a particular thing she finds could make it into an installation at her museum—but she doesn't let that interrupt her gathering. "My mind gives me problems," she said. But when she intentionally relaxes, the objects, artifacts, and ideas that she has found start to form a coherent solution to the problem she's pondering. Very often, she says, "In a dream they gel." What Antonelli does so well is make short-term connections with things that engage her mind when the long-term payoff isn't always apparent. She says that sometimes it takes time and reflection to find the larger meaning and significance of many things she finds.[3]

In this book, I'll show you how to become a curator of inspiration in your life and in your business. If people in business can give themselves permission to hunt and gather ideas and inspiration, all that they've gathered will gel into greater solutions, renewed energy, and purpose. It's that simple.

How This Book Works: The Five M's

Unleashing the creative capacity of each individual in your organization and the teams in which he or she works, while pulling the right organizational levers to keep the whole thing going, is a tricky balancing act. Of course, the solution starts with LAMSTAIH, but that process provides only the broad strokes. We've also developed a framework from which we can work with LAMSTAIH to build the most creative organizations. The framework we use—both in house and with our clients—distills the thinking, behavior, and leadership approach for finding the new ideas that lead to innovation into five key drivers.

1. Mood
2. Mindset
3. Mechanisms
4. Measurement
5. Momentum

Together, these five M's can act as a diagnostic and a road map for changing individuals, empowering teams, and transforming organizations. Focusing your efforts in each of these areas will put you on the path to the change and growth that every business craves. We'll explore each of the M's in great detail in later chapters, but for now, here's a quick overview:

- **Mood** is the attitudes, feelings, and emotions that create the context for inspiration and creativity. Think about it as being like going to a new restaurant or bar—you'll know within a few seconds whether you want to stay there or not. What does it smell like? Are the lights too bright? Are the other patrons too old, too young, too hip, not hip enough? Mood is the mental environment in which people at every level operate and collaborate, and it's something leaders must constantly monitor and adjust.
- **Mindset** is the intellectual foundation of creativity, the baseline capacity each of us has for getting inspired, staying inspired, and thinking differently. In the Mindset chapter, we'll talk about four key thinking disciplines that individuals can use to be inspired at work. Without a shift in mindset toward inspiration, any investment in innovation

will be fruitless. Think of the restaurant again. Is the menu like every other? Does the chef take risks and try new combinations? Is the staff honest in their recommendations?

- **Mechanisms** are the tools and processes of creativity at work. In this section, you'll learn specific tools that will help you engineer inspiration into the way you work, and empower your organization to embrace the kind of behavior that fosters innovation. Restaurants have a variety of mechanisms to help them communicate and be more creative, from the way they greet you and offer you a drink while you wait, to the look and feel of the menu.

- **Measurement** takes into consideration qualitative *and* quantitative performance and provides individuals and organizations with guidance and critical feedback. The type of measures that you put in place at an organizational level send a strong signal of what is important and where people should focus their passion and energy. Thomas Keller, owner and chef of two of the highest-rated restaurants in the world, checks the plates that come back from the dining room to measure how well the food from his kitchen connects with diners. What did they eat? What did they leave untouched?[4]

- **Momentum** in business is pretty much the same as it is in physics: a body at rest stays at rest, and a body in motion stays in motion. Put a little differently, momentum is the active championing and celebrating of inspiration and creativity that creates a self-reinforcing cycle for growing innovation. Momentum is an organizational priority for inspired leaders who have a clear understanding of the other four M's. Do the people who run the restaurant look at you as a one-off transaction, or are they trying to build

Recombobulation Area

Running to catch a flight at MKE, Milwaukee's General Mitchell airport, I came out of the security check, and while gathering my shoes, wrestling with my backpack, and hoping not to disrupt too many people behind me . . . I look up and see a sign that says, Recombobulation Area. How cool is that? In the middle of the conservative Midwest, inside the tightly managed security area, someone in the sign department still had the room inside his or her culture to say, "Let's have a bit of fun." Is your culture promoting this kind of creativity throughout the organization, or do you at least have a few creative catalysts who will take the risk? And when was the last time I ever talked about the Milwaukee airport before I had this experience? Never.

THINK

an ongoing relationship? That might mean asking you to sign up for their e-mail list, sending you coupons and birthday greetings, or introducing you to their produce and dairy suppliers. Those are the kinds of connections that create momentum and keep you coming back.

As you prepare to learn the inspiration discipline, I'd like for you to think of this book as a museum or a gallery with five rooms—one for each M. In those rooms, you'll find a variety of stories, methodologies, and real-world examples of business inspiration in action. I'll be your curator. You can go through the rooms in order, or you can wander about freely. Just make sure you spend some time in each one.

At this point, you should already be questioning what you think you know about inspiration, creativity, and innovation. So take a moment to get yourself recombobulated before we start on the five M's.

CHAPTER 1

Mood

Mood is the attitudes, feelings, and emotions that create the context for innovation and creativity.

ood is one of those you-know-it-when-you-see-it kinds of things. You've probably had the experience of walking into a café, taking a quick look around, and walking right back out. Just didn't feel right. Or you drop off your child at day care, and there's something about all those kids running around that makes you want to sit on the floor and start playing with Legos. That's mood in action. You may not be able to articulate exactly what it is, but you definitely know how it makes you feel. What's a lot less intuitive, though, is the impact mood can have on your creativity. Just think of the last brainstorming session or uninspired team meeting you attended.

You got there at 8:30 sharp, and it was just the two of you—you and the only other person who got there on time. No windows. One of the fluorescent tubes in the ceiling was flickering so faintly that you could barely notice it, but within fifteen minutes, it gave you a pounding headache. One tile in the ceiling had been inexplicably missing for months, and another one had a new brown stain blossoming from its center. The big heavy table was covered in fingerprints, scratches, and faded stains, and all of the chairs were uncomfortable, despite their fancy adjustable features. You knew that one chair was dangerous—lean back in that thing and you'd end up on the floor—but you could never remember which one it was because they all looked the same. The air was stale and still smelled like pepperoni and onions from the prior day's lunch meeting. The trash can was overflowing with lipstick-covered Styrofoam coffee cups and an old box of donuts. The whiteboard was one of those "smart" devices with features that no one remembered how to use. Years ago someone accidentally used a permanent marker on it, and it still said "AGENDA" in bold blue letters in the upper left corner. You tried to communicate to the person sitting across from you, but there was something about the acoustics in the room that smothered words as they came out of your mouth. It was like talking through a pillow. So you sat in silence, waiting for the allotted period of unchecked creativity to begin.

Ah, yes. The conference room. The place where corporate America comes to create. And, sadly, a place we've all been. Fortunately, it doesn't have to be this way. There are ways to change the mood in your organization from an energy suck to something that actually stimulates creativity. And that's exactly what I'm going to show you how to do in this chapter.

Mood is the first of our five M's for a reason: the success or failure of your attempts to inspire your organization and change the way it thinks and operates is often determined long before you begin applying any specific tools or approaches. If you get the mood wrong, you may not even get a chance to try the other drivers of inspiration and innovation, because mood is the foundation for everything else.

There are three very important ways to shift the mood and inspire people within your organization:

- Create purposeful disruptions
- Ask provocative questions and make bold statements
- Make physical changes

Let's take a look at these three mood-changers in detail.

Create Purposeful Disruptions

Deliberately knocking a group's physical and mental dynamics off course, what I call a *purposeful disruption,* is a great mood-altering tool that every leader should use. Keep in mind that there's a very clear difference between an engineered experience that's going to take people out of their current context (like going to a farm to talk about leadership) and a truly spontaneous purposeful disruption. It takes intuition and a healthy tolerance for risk to fully disrupt a moment or interrupt a ritual and shift the mood. But hey, you're a leader: that's your job. Try it out a few times and you'll see the benefits in the renewed energy and passion of your team.

I was saved by a purposeful disruption on the day I got married to Jill.

The St. Francis Borgia Church in Cedarburg, Wisconsin, was packed. I was up at the altar, sweating and trying not to fog up my glasses with the tears of joy I was trying to hold back. I just wanted to get the whole thing going. The violin player had started up, and I could see a glimpse of Jill, looking beautiful at the other end of the church.

Just as Jill was about to make her first step toward me, my Uncle Mitch stood up and addressed the entire group. My heart stopped. Uncle Mitch is a big guy who's pretty much a clone of the Archie Bunker character from the classic television sit-com *All in the Family*. He had on a short, fat tie, and he spoke with a chewed up (and, fortunately, unlit) cigar hanging precariously out of the corner of his mouth.

"Wait a minute! Just hold on here," he exclaimed to the confounded guests. "Aren't we here to get to know each other? Andy would want us to mix it up!"

Mitch hadn't consulted me about this, and, frankly, I really didn't care where people were sitting. I just wanted to get married. From my viewpoint at the front of the church, I could see the danger in Uncle Mitch's call to action. Two women on opposite sides of the aisle were wearing the same dress, and a lot of people were squirming in their seats, unsettled by this off-the-wall request to get up and mingle. Would they actually get along? Would they think my family was good enough? Did they already think we were all as nuts as Uncle Mitch?

There was confusion at first, then nervous laughter. But within just a few moments, Uncle Mitch had everyone up shaking hands with the people around them. After about ten minutes of this mini cocktail party, people gradually found new seats and silently waited for the ceremony to start again. Not only did this purposeful disruption change the guests' mood and their experience of the wedding, but it made the reception an overwhelming success. The families had a jump-start on getting to know each other, and the payoff was exceptional.

Disrupting a ritual can have a powerful effect, but sometimes the best way to influence mood is to create completely *new* rituals. I learned this lesson from one of my former team-mates, a guy named Chip Leon. Chip was always the first person in the office. One day, he decided to try something completely different from his regular morning routine. So he waited in the parking lot until the first of his coworkers drove in. As soon as she stepped out of her car, Chip gave her a standing ovation. The woman was a little taken aback, but after a few seconds she started smiling. On the spot, she and Chip decided to greet the third person to arrive in the same way. Then three of them applauded the fourth, and so on. I'm not going to tell you that these A.M. Cheers (as we call them now) led to any specific inspirational breakthroughs. But I do know that they changed the mood in the office for the rest of the day—all because of one person's spur-of-the moment decision to stir up his morning routine. In fact, A.M. Cheers have been such a success at boosting mood that we now use them as part of our corporate training for new hires. We ask one of the group to leave the room, count to ten, and step back in—to a loud burst of applause.

My team functions as a lab, testing and learning in any capacity that we can. One of our most surprising learning experiences took place in a client session with a Nike executive team. The team members were working toward creating a unified vision and strategy, and they needed a breakthrough to bring them all into alignment. That particular year, budgets were under heavy scrutiny, and each executive had a list of his or her own priorities. The leader of this group knew that collapsing some of the strategies was the most efficient—and effective—way to achieve the organization's broader goals. But to do that, the group members would have to connect as they never had before, so that they could see each other's priorities in a new and fresh way.

We knew that it would take a radical head snap to grab this group's attention. They were successful individually and as a group, so why should they worry about further collaboration? To answer that question, we created an EUK Event (Experience, Understanding, Knowledge—we talk more about these events in Chapter Three, Mechanisms) that would take the group into the field. We met the Nike team at the Ritz-Carlton in Portland over scones and tea, which the group interpreted to mean that they were headed into yet another executive meeting with all the usual dynamics. Then, to their surprise, we told them to join us on the train to Seattle. Once we arrived at the city, we asked everyone in our party to look at more stuff and think about it harder, all in service of seeing themselves as a different kind of working group.

The daylong journey began at the public bus stop. We walked the members of our group up to the corner and handed one of them a full bouquet of Gerbera daisies, with instructions to give the flowers to the first person to step off the incoming bus. The request definitely grabbed the group's attention. When the first rider alighted from the bus, the Nike team member handed her the flowers. As the woman smiled with delight, one of us asked her a simple question: What had she done—that morning, the prior week, or in her lifetime—to deserve this unexpected gift? The woman answered our question with conviction: she was a teacher who had gone through deep budget cuts and yet managed to keep the most critical resources available to her students; she tutored an underprivileged child when she knew the parents could not; for twenty-five years, she had been giving hope to children who might not have gotten it otherwise. With that, she walked off, flowers in hand and head held high.

After taking a minute to process the exchange, we chatted, right there on the corner, about the experience. The Nike executives shared their beliefs about doing the right thing, about how much of what they do goes unnoticed, how they are always trying to do it in the context of the bigger picture, and how they could benefit from more collaboration to get through the driving agendas they all owned. The simple act of recognition for recognition's sake—one question and a handful of flowers—led us to discover how much we all were accomplishing as individuals, but how much more potential there was in the power of collaboration.

On that corner, the members of the executive team developed their new approach to work: more connection to each other, more appreciation of the others' agendas and efforts, and more willingness to ask about and listen to another person's story—things that hadn't been happening at the rate and frequency that they should have been. The team embarked on a new conversation that netted a new outcome.

Later, as we canvassed the tourist area of Seattle, we noticed vendors, shopkeepers, and street musicians with single-stem Gerbera daisies. When we stopped at one busy corner to ask a guitar player where he got his flower, he said, "A woman asked me why I deserved a flower. I told her and she gave it to me... it's a cool day." The ripple effect of this kind of purposeful disruption never ceases to amaze me. Begin with an inspirational act of beauty and watch it cascade through the streets of the city—or your organization.

The words you use, the ways you present yourself—even small details matter, because they all work together to ultimately define the context for creativity and the mood of your organization. Let's look at some examples of how words and

Focus on Who People Are, Not on What They Do

In my view, titles and org charts should be set aside while creating ideas. When I founded Play two decades ago, I wanted to create a different kind of organization, one where the mood for innovation was strong and positive. Over lunch one day, one of my team members at the time, Patty Devlin, suggested that instead of the title of CEO, I call myself the person "In Charge of What's Next." This title sent a clear sign to everyone within the organization and to my clients that my role was not managing and executing—I was there to think ahead and find new opportunities for growth. Today, everyone at Prophet chooses his or her own title. Of course, alternative titles don't change the daily activities we need to do to keep the business running, but they do personalize our approach and start new kinds of conversations.

What message does your current title convey? What title would you choose if you had an option? What title would capture the essence of who you are and the value you deliver to your organization? Come up with a title that expresses that idea—not what you do, but who you are—and then *be* that every second of every day.

THINK

language can transform expectations and change the mood in any organization.

Ask Provocative Questions

A well-placed, provocative question can completely shift the mood of an individual or team by inviting people to think aloud with you. These questions are especially useful in changing the dynamic of a working session. Ideally, they should be abstract or open ended, and the answers shouldn't be easy.

I brought the power of one provocative question to life one day while working on innovation with a global financial institution. I had been working with the company's thirty-member executive team to articulate and outline their five-year innovation strategy. Products, culture, technology, acquisitions, product portfolio, customer segmentation, and organization design were all part of the conversation—as they should have been. But the breadth of the topic had paralyzed the team. As we worked through the conversation, the difficulties became more complex and wiry, as happens so often with an executive team whose members (1) each have an opinion and (2) have years of context informing their point of view.

To move the group forward, I had to unleash the team members' intuition and allow them to "do" rather than "talk." I unleashed them with one question: "So what are you going to do?" With that question lingering in the air, I told them I would return in an hour, and they would report back on the priorities that would set the innovation agenda on its way with full wind in the sails. Upon my return, there was a new energy in the room as the teams huddled around work plans and mind maps. Cutting through the clutter and asking a group of seasoned professionals to "do"—simply to do, not talk—turned their innovation strategy efforts around and unlocked their potential. Never underestimate the power of a simple, provocative question to create a more dynamic, inspirational mood.

Here are some of my favorite provocative questions:

- What's next?
- What don't we know?
- What are we going to do?
- When did you last create something?

- What's relevant?
- What questions should we be asking?
- What's the most important thing?
- What would make you a little more uncomfortable?
- What would be your first move as CEO?
- What is the world telling you?
- How could you put yourself out of business?
- What should we start, stop, and continue?
- How much time have you thought about your team today?
- How much time do you set aside for yourself?
- When is the last time you really looked outside your business, your industry, or your world?
- What's the Bigger Big?
- What could go wrong?
- What could go very right?
- Why should we care?

Make Bold Statements

In addition to asking provocative questions, you can shake up the mood of your organization by creating a forum for bold statements. You want statements that create a little controversy. The statement should fit the topic and objective at hand, while challenging listeners to stretch their thinking. It should also get them to engage you in a discussion instead of just sitting back and listening to (or ignoring) you.

A few years ago, I attended a huge festival for people in the movie business. A famous Hollywood director was one of the keynote speakers. The audience was filled with industry experts and category leaders who had come to hear a legend talk about the film business. The director said many interesting

Whatchathinkin?

You never know where a profound thought can come from. Asking someone, anyone, "Whatchathinkin?" creates a dynamic and participatory environment. It demonstrates that all people and ideas are valued and valid. From a cabbie to a CEO, I never pass up the opportunity to ask, "Whatchathinkin?"

Back in early 2000, I was in an executive meeting for a Silicon Valley tech company. The conversation was going around and around, with each executive essentially posturing for the room by repeating what the previous one had said. There was one person in the meeting who had not spoken up yet, so I pointed to him and asked, "Whatchathinkin?" It turned out that this young man was a junior member sitting in to take notes for an absent executive. Everyone was surprised that I even called on him. But he provided a point of view for the conversation that changed the entire mood of the room. This junior person was in customer service and offered a new perspective on sales and distribution that set a new course of thinking around strategies. A sales perspective on distribution. You never know where a great idea can come from.

Asking your teammates, "Whatchathinkin?" may not yield anything earth-shattering. But then again, it might.

THINK

things, but he made an especially provocative statement when he announced, "The majority of the blockbuster films you'll enjoy in the future—the ones that bring in $200 million—will be made for less than $15 million." Looking around the room, I could tell that the audience members—people who generally don't think twice about dropping $100 million to make a film—were already starting to think about things differently. He had clearly challenged the paradigm. About a year-and-a-half later, the movie *Borat* came out. It cost something like $18 million to make and within months had grossed over $250 million.

Margaret Lewis, the president of Hospital Corporation of America's (HCA's) capital division, completely changed the way I thought about the value of inspiration with this bold statement: "There are no new business strategies." In response to my "What? What do you mean by that?" questions, Margaret explained that modern businesses have figured out all the ways to make things cheaper, faster, and more profitable, and as a result, there aren't any other new ways to do business. Instead, businesses need to rely on *inspiration* as the fuel for informing existing strategies and making them more engaging and productive.

Margaret's bold statement sums up her approach to management, but it also has inspired a change in mood throughout her organization. This simple yet elegant statement has led her teams across the hospital chain to seek out inspiration as a catalyst for changing the way they create and implement business strategies. The people at HCA have not allowed regulatory, financial, legislative, and other constraints to restrict the way they look at the hospital's three core strategic concerns: the emergency room, doctor relationships, and the patient stay. As the teams at HCA continue to add input to the creative equation for each of the organization's strategies, they have developed new and different approaches, which have resulted in better outcomes.[1]

Another example of using a bold statement to reset mood comes from my friend Kent Liffick, formerly of IndyCar racing. Kent is one of the best sports marketers working today, and for a very simple reason: he asks provocative questions, rather than accepting the norms of a very traditional system. Sponsorships have advanced light-years from the early 1980s of radio simulcast, signage, and cross promotions, but most of them continue to be little more than a marketing opportunity gone bad. As a marketer, I seldom see sports sponsorships that absolutely fit and seem to take full advantage of the brand's and the property's assets. When he confronted this problem with IndyCar, Kent asked a big question and got bold results. He asked his client: "If this was the last piece of exposure your company would ever have, what would you do with it?" Knowing that IndyCar is one of the most exotic and exciting sports in the world, Kent was tireless in making sure the sponsors' assets intersected at every touch point. His bold question immediately reframed the challenge that he and his clients were working to resolve, and surrounded that work with a mood of urgency and possibility.[2]

Use Simple Language

Provocative questions and bold statements don't require flowery language in order to effectively shift mood. Anita Roddick, founder of the Body Shop, told me two things that continue to serve as mechanisms to inspire thinking within her company—and that are excellent examples of the power of simple language. She shared the first idea with me over dinner in a French restaurant in Denmark. We were talking about passion and how important it is for driving change in any organization. When I asked her why that was so, she replied, "Passion persuades." Later, at London's Heathrow Airport, I told Anita that she was the most inspiring person I'd ever known. When I asked her to give me one last piece of advice before I boarded my plane back to Virginia, she replied with another simple statement: "Words create the world." Anita has since passed away, but I will always be grateful to her for the gift of passion and the bold and powerful ideas she shared with me in such simple but eloquent words.[3]

"Passion persuades." "Words create the world." The messages of these simple sentences are incredibly important. There is nothing more powerful for creating change than passion. Passion is the fuel that gives ideas power and makes any organization run. At the same time, words are the tools we use to express our passion and our ideas, so it's critical that every leader be purposeful with words. Together, both of Anita's comments have helped me create better things throughout my career—and have helped me help my clients do the same.

Take John Unwin, for example. John is a special CEO. He has twenty-five years of hotel and resort management experience that includes running Caesar's Palace and the San Francisco Fairmont. He helped guide Ian Schrager's hotels, and today serves as CEO of The Cosmopolitan of Las Vegas, a unique luxury resort in the heart of the Las Vegas Strip. John has genuine passion, *real* passion, that he has transferred to his team—and his business. Talk about a resort that is going to change its category. Rooms with expansive, one-of-a-kind private terraces that allow guests to step outside and take in sweeping views of the Las Vegas skyline are just one of the amazing offerings that set this property apart.

We helped John and his team launch the new resort brand to his top 150 employees months before the opening. To provide John with the perfect backdrop to kick off the event, we picked the Neon Museum, ten minutes down the expressway from the Strip. The museum's "boneyard" holds the cast-off neon signs from every major hotel, casino, and other establishment in Vegas—the Silver Slipper, the Golden Nugget, the Stardust, and so on. We drove the group to the site of this glittering collection in three fifty-passenger buses and then gathered them around John to hear him tell his story. And he did it beautifully. With dozens of giant neon signs as his backdrop, John jumped up on a rickety picnic table and talked about one of his first experiences in Las Vegas—the magical evening he spent in the legendary Bacchanal Room in Caesar's Palace. John's words painted a picture of old Vegas that sparked his team's imagination as they prepared to help create the next chapter in the city's history and to make The Cosmopolitan a leader in its industry. These 150 people stood riveted because of John's conviction, his humor, realness, and passion for change—change that would encompass an industry and a city, not just a resort.

After John finished his talk, we bused the group back to The Cosmopolitan, which was still under construction. There, we gathered the first 150 members of The Cosmopolitan team in a circle in the hotel's unfinished ballroom, and, in a symbolic moment, we handed out markers and asked them to remove their hard hats, sign them, and pass them to the next person for his or her signature. When everyone's hat had made its way around the circle, it held the signature of every person in the group—colleagues who were about to embark on an amazing journey along with John. The full rotation took an awkward twenty-two minutes, and at one point, I became concerned that the group was growing restless. But when I tried to cut it short, John told me to let it roll. This was a part of the journey we had laid out, and he wanted to use it to fire their passion and to emphasize—149 times—their role in this collective venture. John's magical touch shines through in these moments, which people remember and use as a guiding beacon. John's passion persuades his team to always look for meaningful change. And they will. I'm convinced.[4]

Take a minute and think about the language you use on a day-to-day basis and the impact it has on the mood of your organization. What underlying meanings might you be communicating to your group, and how do they shape your ability to communicate on an authentic level? Can you change the way you and your team interact by saying what you actually mean? Do you succumb to corporate-speak? Are you sacrificing inspiration for efficiency?

Make Physical Changes

Perhaps the easiest (and cheapest) way to start setting or shifting your team's mood is simply to go somewhere else. Now, I know that the idea of changing the physical environment to change thinking is hardly a new one, but keep these two ideas in mind:

1. The three-dimensional environment is only half of the equation—probably the less important half. The other part, which I'll get to in the next chapter, is mental.
2. When you're thinking about alternative surroundings for working with your team, you've got to get beyond the traditional nature walks and sporting events. Push yourself a little. It's okay, go ahead.

A few years ago, we were hired by a financial services company whose leaders wanted to find out why their employees weren't thinking big enough. Situated in a typical suburban office park, the company designated each of its many buildings by number—"Building 1," "Building 2," and so on—

expressing a lack of personality that's never an encouraging sign when a company claims creativity as an organizational value.

As I walked through the parking lot toward the entrance, I was almost bowled over by a stream of employees on their way out. It was close to noon on a beautiful, sunny day, so I naturally assumed they were all in a hurry to enjoy their time off—parks, healthy walks, you know, get some fresh air. Turns out, most of them weren't actually going anywhere. Instead, they got into their cars and stayed there, unpacking their bag lunches, drinking soda, reading books, and listening to the radio. Were things really so bad inside that employees had to flee to their cars to find some peace? (The whole scene reminded me of a poem I once read in which the poet talks about people leaving their car windows cracked when they go into work—not in an effort to keep the car cool, but because they leave 75 percent of themselves behind when they go in to work, and want to be sure that a part of them can still breathe.)

As I entered Building 2, I began to understand the exodus to the parking lot. The walls were dark and cold, the floors were dark and cold, and the furniture was dark and cold. The security guard looked up from his bag of fried pork rinds just long enough to ask me to sign in, and I noticed that right behind him, bolted to the wall, was the only bit of color in the place: a bright red defibrillator—the one thing in the building guaranteed to get your heart going. What a metaphor. The pall extended to the graveyard of cubicles inside, which remained absolutely silent even after the lunch crowd returned. All around me, there were people with their heads down, hushed conversations, closed doors. Not a sound anywhere. I broke out my pack of Bubblicious gum, and when I started noisily unwrapping a piece, heads spun toward me as if I'd set off a grenade. How could anyone find inspiration in that dead zone?

Other companies understand the link between environment and creativity, and one great example is GE. GE is all
about leadership, and has been for years. Today, the company
continues to write new chapters in the book of global corporate
leadership. Susan Peters, the chief learning officer and one of
my longest-standing business crushes (more on those crushes
later), has helped define and shape leadership at GE over the
course of the organization's many iterations. Susan has an
uncanny combination of intelligence and intuition, and she is,
without a doubt, one of the strongest strategic "people-based"
executives I've ever worked with. Susan knew that Crotonville,
the GE corporate development center famed for its best-in-
class executive leadership, helps define leadership at GE and
around the world. So when she began reimagining the Crotonville campus, Susan asked my team to help. She wanted to
create a new look and feel for every aspect of the campus—its
environment, experience, content, and other assets.[5]

Big projects start with a big vision, but they really begin
taking shape through small actions. We developed work teams
to address a number of needs for the new campus, such as
more opportunities to network, new technology, and creative
and fun evening activities. The teams also activated a number
of quick-win ideas, such as offering global newspapers in the
lobbies and new technology in the guest rooms. But it all came
to life when we added a few coats of paint and a makeshift desk
in one of the Crotonville administrative offices. My teammates
Barry Saunders, Hillary deRoo, and Lauren Mirsky had been
spending quite a bit of time at the campus and were in need
of a work area. In keeping with the laboratory mentality we
were trying to instill in the Crotonville team, we worked with
the campus facilities team to design an eight-by-ten-foot room

that would be a lively standout in a sea of tan offices. Picture it: bright green walls (one gallon of paint at $14.00); yellow sawhorses from Lowes ($25.00 each) supporting an eight-foot board (salvaged from the maintenance department) and five high stools ($26.00 each). And the fancy accessory? Five elbow-bending white lights affixed to the table ($7.99 per light).

As we set up camp in the new office, ready to begin a week of reinvention and discovery, a flood of Crotonville teammates streamed in to tell some story or express some opinion about the room. They said the seats were too high but might be interesting; the green walls were too loud, but full of energy; the desk was too raw, but screamed to have ideas generated on it; the lights were too dull, but might be a good effect for late-night dream sessions. The room sparked a debate. A conversation. A point of view. It was the farthest thing the Crotonville team could imagine from the typical L-shaped desk and credenza—and that was the point. That thirty-minute Monday-morning conversation became the catalyst to spark the team's thinking about the rest of the fifty-nine acres and all its amazing facilities. A physical change that cost a few hundred dollars helped inspire us to think about the entire project with more energy and passion. Small physical changes helped people see possibilities and have a fresh conversation.

Shake Up People—Even the Creatives

Not long ago, my colleague Ben Armbruster and I met with a team of executives from Disney. Our first meeting was at our office loft, which is dynamic, interactive, and deliberately designed to encourage creativity and inspiration. But Disney's offices are too (after all, they *are*) Disney. So to shake things up a bit, Ben grabbed a flipchart, an easel, and a handful of markers and announced that we were going to move the whole group to the nearby Hollywood cemetery—which has nothing to do with the film industry, but is a very famous cemetery in Richmond, Virginia, named long ago for its many holly trees. To his great credit, Disney executive Duncan Wardle said, in his inimitable British accent, "Right-o, lads, off we go!" and we relocated to the South's version of "Hollywood," where we spent the next six hours talking—quite productively—about how Disney could do things differently.[6]

Duncan and another Disney cast member, Victoria Finn, later referred to the cemetery trip as "forced reflection."[7] It made us all step back, pause, and create great things. Over the course of the next two years, I helped Disney's Creative Inc. team put inspirational and unexpected locations at the heart of its creative ideation and transform the company's approach to building great ideas. I have joined the Disney team at a graffiti studio in Los Angeles, where we tagged a wall in the alley, and I have watched them interact with children in afterschool tutoring programs and foster homes. That moment in the cemetery was a wake-up call to the creative ideation team at Disney, reminding them that even an organization with a decidedly creative output could benefit from shifting the mood of their internal operation.

Change Your Physical Identity to Change the Way You Think

Physically taking people outside their normal frame of reference can offer tremendous insight into the way those people think. We worked with a major credit card company looking for new ways to market products to people who have poor (or no) credit—students, immigrants, people who might have had a bankruptcy or two under their belt, and so on. Judging from the cars that pulled up in front of our building, we were pretty sure that no one on the team was in that particular demographic. Most of them had no clue what it was like to live paycheck to paycheck or to have to choose between paying an overdue credit card bill or buying groceries.

Our engagement with them started out like any other corporate meeting—pastries and coffee, State of the Union, introductions. Then we ushered everyone downstairs, where a loud, rumbling city bus was waiting. Judging from the wide eyes and puzzled expressions, I think it's safe to say that very few of the folks on the team had ever been on a city bus. Nevertheless, we piled in and headed to a thrift store. We gave each person on the bus $20 and told them that they had to go inside the store and buy themselves an outfit to wear for the rest of the day. At first they thought we were kidding, but the resolute look on our team members' faces said otherwise.

Thirty minutes later, we were back on the bus. Everyone, including our team, wore his or her new clothes for the rest of the day as we talked to consumers, followed new routines, and explored what it means to live at the bottom of the financial pyramid. (Well, not everyone: in an interesting twist, one agency partner took a different approach, and instead bought one of the thrift store mannequins, which he carried around with him for the rest of the day.) The pure inspiration that came from altering our physical appearance gave the group a tactile, experiential, and three-dimensional insight into the client's customer base and allowed the company to create a very successful set of new products and offerings.

Build It Right, or They Might Not Come

Another way to use our three-dimensional surroundings to shift mood is to set aside (or, if you've got the budget, to specially build) innovation areas. But be careful. Even though our physical working environment clearly has a major impact on our behavior and interactions, it's not magic.

One Fortune 100 client of ours set up a gorgeous outdoor area for meetings and conversations, hoping to energize the staff and trigger fresher ideas. The idea was a good one, but it wasn't well executed. The new "innovation area" was right outside the windows of the company's C-suite. No one on the staff wanted to use the area, for fear that the senior execs would look out and think they were loafing in the sun. Eventually, the abandoned area became a symbol for "nice idea, bad execution."

A few years ago, one of our clients was excited to show us the brand-new innovation areas they'd spent more than $2 million to build within their eighty-thousand-square-foot facility. The new areas were strategically located in the center of every floor and were appointed with flat-screen monitors, magazines for inspiration, electronic whiteboards, snacks, drinks, and funky furniture that screamed, "Sit on me and be creative!" The problem? Tacked to the wall next to one of the entrances was a crude, handwritten sign that said, "Please be quiet. People are working." Not surprisingly, that innovation area—and all the other ones I looked at—were empty. Clearly, the prevailing attitude in the company was that working and having a conversation in an innovation area were mutually exclusive activities, and that "value delivery" meant sitting quietly at a desk. *Boy, I thought, have we got a long way to go . . .*

Segregated innovation areas can have a negative effect on an organization's mood. They can give people the impression that innovation is supposed to happen only in specific "corrals." If people walk by and the areas are empty, the whole organization can begin to feel devoid of life and creativity. And if your attitudes and policies contradict the atmosphere of innovation, you just waste time and money by setting up special spaces for

Have You Ever Had a Drink?

I was driving through Phoenix, the top of my rental convertible down, in the blazing heat of summer, when I developed a craving for a cold Margarita. I found a Mexican dive and had a great drink. I saw behind the bar a page from a magazine that listed "nine places that you have to have a drink." I copied down the list, and so far, I've checked off seven of them. All that's left are numbers 7 and 8. Part of the reason I want to work my way through the list is for the drinks. But I also want to experience the places and meet the people who gather there. Take a look at the list. Each place has its own unique mood to absorb:

1. A Sidecar at the St. James Hotel in London
2. A Mint Julep at the Pendennis Club at Louisville on Derby Day
3. A Gimlet at any sleazy lounge in LA
4. A Coke at the San Diego Zoo
5. A gin and tonic at the Mandarin Club overlooking Columbus Circle in Manhattan
6. A spiked lemonade at Prune on the Lower East Side of Manhattan
7. A Sazerac at Smith and Mills in Tribeca in Manhattan
8. A Bellini at the San Piedro hotel in Positano, Italy
9. A Stroh's beer in the bleachers at Tiger Stadium in Detroit

Each drink is special because of the unique context in which I enjoy it, whether it's drinking it where it's made or enjoying the sheer ubiquitous anonymity of an LA lounge. You should create a list of your own experiences and explore as many moods as possible.

THINK

innovation instead of trying to instill a creative atmosphere and mood throughout the organization. It's like giving someone the title of "creative director," which promotes the misguided idea that only one person in the organization has a responsibility for creativity.

In real life, creativity doesn't usually happen while you're sitting alone at a desk. In fact, distractions and working with other people are critical ingredients. Donna Sturgess, the former global head of innovation for GlaxoSmithKline, calls it "blue noise," and uses it to gauge her company's mood. Unlike the white noise of heads-down working, blue noise is a symphony of creativity, the audible sound of energy, collaboration, and curiosity in action.[8] Blue noise can happen anywhere—the chance meeting at the coffeemaker; the team lunch; the overheard conversation that sparks a new thought. Every moment that you or your people aren't interacting is a missed opportunity for creating.

The moral? Before you start making any physical changes, be damned sure that everyone in your organization—from the top down—is ready to make the leap. And challenge your ideas, to be certain that no symbols, titles, words, or artificial limitations get in the way of your efforts to recharge mood by reimagining physical spaces.

Become the CMO (Chief Mood Officer)

In 2009, when we sold Play to Prophet, the *Richmond Times-Dispatch,* our local newspaper, reported on the story. That by itself isn't particularly impressive. But the next day, I received an envelope with a copy of the article and a personalized note saying, "Great news!" from Tom Silvestri, a good friend who's also the paper's publisher. Receiving that article made me smile for the rest of the day, and in some small way, boosted the mood of the rest of my team too. A few days later I happened to be at an event that Tom was attending, and I went over and thanked him for sending the article, telling him how much I appreciated that he took the time out of what must be an insanely busy schedule. He told me that he actually does it every day. "People are always saying they don't want to read the paper because there's never any good news. That's simply not true. There are good-news stories every day. And I consider it part of my job to share the news." Now *that* was impressive. So much so that I've started clipping out good-news articles about people or companies I know and sending them along with a quick "Great news!" note.[9]

Tom helped me stumble on to one of the great lessons of leadership—one you won't find on any list of the top traits of effective leaders. It's simply this: part of your job description is setting the mood in your organization. Good mood leads to good environment. Good environment creates a good workplace. And a good workplace is where people want to stay. It doesn't get any better than that.

In 2001, I was in Austin, Texas, visiting GSD&M, the maverick advertising shop. Normally I travel with at least one of my teammates. But that night in Austin, I was all alone. It was late. I'd been traveling across the country all day, thanks to a four-hour delay on the last leg. I decided to distract and reward myself with a big meal. So I asked the concierge at my hotel, "Where can I get a delicious meal for, say, a hundred dollars? I want to spoil myself." She recommended a place right around the corner from the hotel.

I walked in, optimistic and hungry. The joint smelled pretty good. The lighting was nice—low but not too low.

The place had lots of dark wood paneling; cool, modern furnishings; and an overall good vibe. It seemed the perfect place for a guy eating alone. "Table for one, please," I said to the maitre d'.

To my shock, he let out a barely audible "Tsk tsk," as from behind his little podium he took in my wrinkled, well-traveled clothes. He snatched up a menu, barked "Follow me," and whisked off into the dining room.

I hustled after him as he snaked through the maze of tables and rooms. It was Monday night, and the place was pretty much empty. The whole time we were walking, I kept thinking, *Is that my table? Is that my table?* But it never was. My anticipation quickly turned to disappointment when he stopped in front of a tiny, dark table in a back corner next to the kitchen door.

Sorry—that just wasn't going to work for me. I wasn't going to sit there, turned sideways, deliberately staring at a blank wall so I wouldn't have to watch the guy washing dishes. No way. Before the maitre d' had a chance to patronizingly say, "Here we are, sir," I grabbed the menu right out of his hands and looked him right in the face.

"No. No. You follow me," I said as I sped back through the restaurant. I chose a seat at the bar, which was open and airy and located right in the middle of all the action, not lost in some dank corner. Now *that* was a proper place to have a nice meal. A place where I could look at more stuff.

Before long, I was having the time of my life chatting with the bartender, watching the Yankees game on the TV above the bar, talking about how much we both loved New York. I found out that he's Croatian. My family is from Serbia, so we talked about our grandparents, their struggles as immigrants, and all the sacrifices those before us had made to build such a great melting pot of a country. I vividly remember the meal I had that evening: mushroom risotto, freshly baked bread, a few Pilsner Urquells, and a great sampler of sorbets for dessert.

Too often we're told where to sit, what to do, how to act. And too often we blindly go along with the program. But we don't have to—at least not all the time. Consider yourself the CMO (chief mood officer) and take control of setting and reframing the mood at your organization. "No. No. You follow me" is a very powerful phrase. Try it out. To be clear, the point is not that you are demanding that people actually follow you. Rather, it's that you don't have to take what you are given when it comes to mood. Instead, take control of your own experience in life and business to create the right mood.

Okay, Now You Try . . .

Before we move on to the next M, Mindset, take a minute to think about the mood of your organization and its ability to inspire creativity and innovation. Ask yourself these questions:

- How many people are smiling as you walk through the halls?
- What percentage of doors are closed? open?
- Are you surprised and delighted at work on a monthly, weekly, or daily basis?
- What time of day do you have a corporate laugh?
- What would happen if you wore name tags that announce your daily mood?

CHAPTER 2

Mindset

Mindset is the intellectual foundation of creativity, the baseline capacity each of us has for getting inspired, staying inspired, and thinking differently.

There are millions of possible ways to find inspiration in the workplace. However, having worked with thousands of people in corporations all over the world, we have identified four behaviors that are absolutely essential to becoming—and staying—inspired. Together, these four acts, which we call "thinking disciplines," produce a creative, inspired mindset:

1. Change your perspective
2. Take risks
3. Find your passion
4. Challenge assumptions and embrace ambiguity

In this chapter, we're going to take a closer look at what it takes to develop your willingness and ability to accomplish these four thinking disciplines and, in the process, develop Mindset, the second of the five M's. The best way to understand Mindset is to jump right in.

Change Your Perspective to Open Your Mind

No, this isn't a case of déjà vu all over again. In the previous chapter we talked about making physical changes to your environment and perspective. Now we're focusing exclusively on *mental* changes—more specifically, on the sources you go to when you're seeking inspiration.

Changing your perspective is really all about your openness to new perspectives, situations, or ideas. It relates to your comfort and ability to incorporate alternative points of view when generating new ideas. It also indicates your general interest and curiosity about things. The ability to change perspective allows you to be open to a greater variety of ideas and viewpoints while finding solutions.

Some sources—like getting to know your customer and asking your employees for suggestions—are so simple and obvious that you'll be tempted to kick yourself for not having explored them sooner. Let me give you a couple of more detailed examples.

Ask a Completely New Audience for Ideas

The Volvo Your Concept Car (YCC) was unveiled in 2004 after three years of research and development.[1] Volvo realized that when it comes to buying a car, the vast majority of purchasing decisions are made by women. But Volvo's products were being designed almost entirely by men. Volvo saw an opportunity to innovate by exploring women's preferences, so it formed an all-female design team.

The team's new design had many innovative features, such as:

- A hood that was designed to be opened only by a mechanic. Volvo's studies showed that women didn't care for working under the hood, so the team designed a transmission that needs service only about every thirty thousand miles. The car sends a radio signal to the nearest dealership when it's time to bring it in, so the dealer can call the car's owner and tell her that it's due for service.

- Theater-style back seats. The seats are generally in the "up" position, which leaves lots of floor space for shopping bags and boxes.

- More easily cleaned interiors and exteriors. The upholstery and carpeting are removable and washable. Like Teflon-coated cookware, the paint has no-stick properties for easier maintenance.

- Buttons and control mechanisms collected in one central location. All the controls are in one place, rather than scattered all over the steering wheel and other locations.

- A "capless" gas tank. Women found dealing with the gas cap a nuisance, so the designers adopted the same capless ball valve technology used in racing vehicles, which allows drivers to put the gas nozzle directly into the car. No cap handling needed.

- A ton of storage space. A large central compartment is sized to fit a laptop bag, and a special compartment in the doorjamb holds wet umbrellas.

- Automatically opening doors. The gull-wing door you are closest to fully opens when you push the button on the key fob. No need to put your bags down on the ground to open the door.

Volvo's YCC team uncovered many opportunities for innovation by deliberately changing their perspectives and looking to an unconventional design team for ideas. (Do you think that a male team would create headrests with a slit for ponytails?) Although many of the features of the YCC car were inspired by traditionally female-centric environments or habits, overall the innovations are universal in appeal and function. As Marti Barletta, an expert on female consumer patterns, noted in an article at autointell.com: "If you meet the expectations of women, you exceed the expectations of men."[2]

The YCC project wasn't a typical piece of intellectual market research, and there was no science or data behind it. It was truly innovation that evolved because someone trusted her intuition over intelligence. As it turns out, the YCC was never actually produced. But by going through the exercise, Volvo completely changed the way it talked—and appealed—to women.

My team has seen how trusting instinct can open up new perspectives and encourage innovation. A few years ago, we organized an event that we called Exchange, in which we brought in ten of our biggest clients from all over the world and immersed them in creative experiences. They painted murals, cooked, wrote poetry, did executive coaching, and much more—fresh activities that opened up fresh perspectives into the process of innovation. Over lunch on the last day, we asked all the participants to tell us the most important thing they learned about innovation. A reply from Ivy Ross, executive VP at Gap, sums up the message we heard from all of them: "Our companies have stopped trusting our instincts and have made innovation much too complicated."[3] That kind of mindset anchors organizations to the past, rather than driving them into the future.

Look for New Perspectives from All Three Sources of Inspiration

So far, I've been talking about using people as sources of inspiration. But inspiration can come from a lot of other sources. If you've got the time and the budget, you may pack your bags and travel the world to find compelling insights around an important topic. Or you might have just fifteen minutes to spend in front of your computer. Either way, part of having a creative, inspired mindset is learning to look at more stuff in a variety of places. There are three broad sources of inspiration that you should think of as a continuum:

- **Direct** sources of inspiration are the easy, obvious, and expected ones that are directly related to the topic at hand—things like market data, competitive analysis, and, as we discussed earlier, talking to your customers and employees. For example, if your job is to reinvent a line of clothing to make it more comfortable, your direct source of inspiration might come from spending time making head-to-head comparisons between your jackets, pants, and dresses and those made by your competitors.
- **Tangential** sources are, as the name implies, not directly related to your topic. In our clothing line example, you might explore how the concept of comfort plays out in other consumer areas, such as footwear, furniture, eyeglasses, and so on. You might find insights for your

objective based on the marketing, positioning, or construction of these tangential sources.

- **Abstract** sources are ones that on the surface seem completely unrelated to your objective. The connection might be metaphorical, random, or nonexistent. For example, what could a telemarketer learn from a suicide hotline operator? They both need to make quick connections over the phone. How could riding shotgun in a race car help a computer engineer make a better user interface for his software? Software users and race car drivers both want speed and functionality at the same time.

Of the three sources of inspiration, abstract connections not only generate the most novel ideas (usually because they're typically the first time a concept has "jumped the fence" out of your industry) but also are the most fun to seek out. But be warned: this kind of discovery is addictive.

The 2006 Red Dot international design awards provide a great example of abstract connections in action. Among the winners, there were only two U.S. companies. One, of course, was Apple, nominated for the iPod Nano. But you probably never heard of the other one: LoggerHead Tools, creators of the Bionic Wrench, an innovative blend of pliers and the adjustable wrench.[4] The Bionic Wrench eliminates the need to carry around a ton of different tools because it adjusts to fit many sizes. The way that it grips also makes stripping nuts and bolts less likely.

The inspiration for the design didn't come from the world of wrenches or any other tools. It came from a camera lens. The engineer who designed the tool is also an amateur photographer, and the spark came to him while watching the way that shutters and lenses close in toward the center.

Like all inspired innovations, this design came about through understanding the power of connections—seeing something new or looking at something familiar in a new way.

To give you a bit more insight into how looking for inspiration in direct, tangential, and abstract sources plays out in real life, I've put together a chart with a sampling of projects we have been asked to work on (see next page). For each objective, the chart lists the places where we found new perspectives in each of the three sources of inspiration.

Explore Sources of Inspiration That Are Close to Home

Regardless of how big or small your company is, your most valuable assets are the varied experiences of your team and the perspectives they bring to any situation. To encourage divergent thinking, create opportunities to solicit input from your team when generating ideas. More important, incorporate their thinking into the ideas you're working on.

As you may know, GE's corporate mantra is "imagination at work." Well, in 2007, GE hired us to uncover innovative examples of how "imagination at work" was coming to life within the organization, and the company's top management wanted to announce the results of our work to their global leadership team at GE's annual summit. Our solution? Well, in keeping with our fanatical obsession with documenting everything (often in unusual ways), we mailed out disposable video cameras to a handful of GE employees in every region of the world and asked them to tell their stories.

One story came back from an industrial unit, where managers had spent several months and hundreds of thousands

Objective	Direct	Tangential	Abstract
Hotel loyalty program	Concierge Maintenance staff Travel agent Executive assistants handling travel and expenses Business traveler	Museum annual memberships Retail-affiliated credit cards Gym memberships Cell phone plans	Family relationships Sports fan sites and clubs University alumni National pride and historic preservation societies, like DAR
Big-box customer experience	Service center Checkout line Warehouse Supply chain Competitors Alongside mom	Mall designer or commercial engineer Museum curator Mapmaker	Police department, missing persons School for the blind Parade organizer
Plumbing fixtures	Outdoor pool Designer kitchen Homes	Gym locker room or spa Greenhouse Water treatment plant	City park Dance studio Kite maker
Hygiene products for teens	Gym locker room Home bathrooms Backpacks College fraternity houses	Dermatologist Teen magazine reporter Perfumery	Bakery Candy company Greenhouse

Technology and educational services for health care	Nursing stations Ambulance ride-along Private medical offices	Learning development centers Auto mechanic	Translator Orchestra conductor Control tower operator
Redesign the bra	Fabric manufacturer All ages of women Retail store	Hardware store Mountain climber Interior designer Personal trainer	Aquarium Women's rights and support groups Florist
New product development for an energy drink	Sodas and other energy drinks	Vitamins and supplements	Motivational speakers Amusement park thrill rides Nuclear power plants
DVD retail purchase experience	Blockbuster Video	Amazon.com Public library Barnes & Noble	Wine shop
Corporate environment promoting creativity	Google headquarters	Guggenheim Museum	Kindergarten classroom Baltimore Aquarium

of dollars creating a plan to redesign one of their manufacturing plants to make it more efficient. Once the plans were presented to the workforce that actually ran the equipment, one of the operators pointed out that they didn't need to reengineer the whole plant at all. All they had to do was move two pieces of equipment a little closer together.

And that's what they did. No massive overhaul, just a simple tweak suggested by someone on the front lines. Had those managers not reached out to get some input from end users (in this case, their own people), they would have most likely spent a lot more time and money implementing a plan that didn't need to be implemented. Like GE, you can develop a mindset that's open to the smartest, simplest, and most effective innovations by gaining the input and perspectives of the people closest to your operation.

Learn from Random People

Learn to look beyond focus groups in your search for valuable insights. A few years ago, Trustmark, a midsize Chicago-based financial services company, needed to know more about its customers. The company's research teams had done a ton of quantitative market research, but weren't getting the insights they needed. I suggested that they simply go out and talk to consumers. No focus groups. No research department. Just take the entire senior leadership team down to Navy Pier and start chatting up regular people.

During the bus ride down to the city, the CEO, Dave McDonough, made it clear that he believed we already had all the research we needed, but agreed to invest a day in the process. By the end of the afternoon, his view was completely transformed by the valuable information his team had gathered from people strolling through Navy Pier. Not long after that, he established a program to take other teams from the organization out to talk with real consumers.[5]

When I think about the power of "random" perspectives, I remember the day my parents dropped me off at college. I was intimidated by all of the upperclassmen playing Frisbee on the lawn and pumping music from boom boxes in windows. Dad moved into advice mode; he put his hand on my shoulder, pointed to the ivy-covered buildings, and said, "Andy, 90 percent of what you learn here is not going to be in any of those classrooms." He was dead-on. More than just a paycheck (or diploma), *the value we take away from every job (and college too) is the people we meet and relationships we form.* Inspired, innovative leaders understand the value of such random insights, too. They're constantly adjusting their mindset by changing their perspective and making connections outside their industries and culture.

The Human Library

In Malmo, Sweden, the local public library has an unusual feature. Visitors interested in learning about different minority groups can "check out" someone from the "living library." Whether he or she is an animal rights activist, a transgendered individual, a gypsy, or a lesbian, the person makes himself or herself available for one-on-one conversation.

If you're working with a team or a group that needs to look at more stuff, but time, location, or resources prevent you from going out into the world, consider creating your own human library. It's a great way to bring inspiration to life, especially tangential and abstract sources of inspiration.

THINK

Engage Your Loyal Opposition

One very effective and efficient way of forcing yourself to expand your perspective and shift your mindset is to find your *loyal opposition*. Leaders tend to surround themselves with people who think like they do. Unfortunately, those people too often tell leaders what they *think* the leaders want to hear instead of what they really *need* to hear. Your loyal opposition won't fall into that trap. They're fiercely true to you, but they'll give it to you straight and provide you with honest, new insights.

When identifying your loyal opposition, look for people who think differently than you do. These people might include a coworker down the hall, someone you met at a conference, your spouse, a competitor, the UPS guy, the babysitter, or the young woman with the tattoos and tongue piercings who makes your morning cappuccino. The only requirement for inclusion in the group is a willingness to give you straight feedback, with no sugarcoating.

Incorporating the points of view from this loyal opposition into your thinking can be a humbling experience, but don't take it personally. Take it professionally. Having a loyal opposition is especially important for people who consider themselves (or are considered by others) creative and intelligent. As my wife says, "Creative, intelligent people are very good at convincing themselves of just about anything."

Think About Your Perspective

Now that you've taken a look at the various ways to change your organization's perspective, take a moment to answer these questions and gauge your current mindset as it applies to changing perspectives—and be honest.

- What is most important to you and why?
- When it's time to create ideas, whom do you go to first?
- Imagine yourself at eighteen. What would that person tell you today?
- Where do the good ideas come from within your company or team?
- What relationships are you in that challenge you? Why are they challenging?
- What do you do? Who are you?
- If you could change a routine in your schedule, what would you change?
- How would other people describe your degree of predictability?

Skin Your Knees

How likely are you to take risks when generating and promoting new ideas? Risks are framed and measured in terms of perceived gains or losses in relation to possible outcomes. For example, you may think, "If I share this idea, will people look at me like I'm crazy?" As we've seen earlier in this book, fear—of failure, criticism, or simply the uncertainty of the unknown—is one of the biggest censors of ideas within teams. As a catalyst for creative thinking, you should create a safe environment for idea generation that does not immediately judge or ridicule ideas. In other words, you need to be willing to skin your knees, and your team needs to know that you expect them to do the same. Developing a mindset that encourages calculated risk-taking will help ensure that you and your organization are constantly developing new, divergent ideas from which to draw solutions.

Think of the *Worst* Possible Idea

Sometimes the worst ideas generate the most inspired innovations. In 2002, a major U.S. toy company came to my team with two goals: to develop creative capabilities and to explore new ideas for its successful doll. I wanted to start off our discussions with something kind of zingy, so I asked the large group of marketing professionals who lived and breathed the product a simple question: "What is the *worst* idea for reinventing this doll?" Blank stares. In a world dedicated to creating profitable products, this sort of request is a real stumper. After a minute of silence, I offered an idea of my own: "What if she were a prostitute?" After a lot of nervous laughter and a few raised eyebrows, the team got what I was trying to do, and the ideas began to flow.

Over the next couple of hours, we explored the idea of the doll as a hooker, and, as each idea built on the ones before, we began talking about the doll by moonlight. The doll's existing backstory—her activities, friends, accessories, and doll life—was rooted in daytime. Her after-dark life, though, was completely new territory.

It would have been easy (even sensible) to laugh off the streetwalker concept, but spending some time deliberately pursuing ill-conceived ideas opened up a whole new path of creative possibilities. Today, thanks to a rotten idea, the doll's life is filled with limos, nightclubs, new fashions, and dance parties.

It's a lot easier to *tell* people to take risks than to actually take them yourself. Modern business is designed to engineer risk out of the equation as much as possible. But taking risks actually shifts your mindset and boosts your creativity. The first time that you take a chance and fail miserably, and the world doesn't come crashing down on top of you, you realize that it is possible to succeed through failure. You also start developing risk tolerance.

Celebrate Risk-Taking

For my team, a skinned knee—the result of taking risks—is a badge of honor. You tried. You gave it everything you had. You got knocked down and got a little hurt, but you got up and kept playing. When it comes to risk, no one is more important than a strong leader who sets the tone and creates a culture where people can walk around with scraped-up knees.

I heard a story years ago that a senior leader at Ore-Ida, a Heinz subsidiary known especially for frozen potato products, called his senior engineers together and issued a challenge: take risks, don't be afraid to fail, and deliver some innovative new products. He couldn't have been clearer. But as the weeks went by, the leader wasn't getting any results. His people were simply too risk averse (and remember, we're talking about frozen potatoes here).

So the leader went out to an Army-Navy surplus store and bought a cannon. That's right, a large piece of military artillery, which he placed on the front lawn of Ore-Ida's corporate campus. He gathered the same engineers together and made them a promise. If any one of them were to have a "perfect failure," he would let him or her shoot the cannon. He defined a perfect failure as identifying a good idea, researching it, testing it, and taking it as far as possible before coming to the realization that it should be canned.

Well, before too long, Ore-Ida was having perfect failure parties around the cannon. You can imagine what it must feel like to be working away in your cubicle, frustrated, worrying about rejection, struggling to make an idea work—and then hearing that cannon go off. It signals that it's okay to fail, as long as you're giving it your all. And don't forget about the leader. Going out and buying a cannon so your team will understand you're serious about taking risks is a fantastic risk in itself—one that has since paid off. Could the leader's idea have failed? Absolutely. But he gave a culture-shattering sign that he was just fine with that.[6]

Okay, so you get the idea that going out there and skinning your knees is a good thing. Unfortunately, corporate America isn't set up to deal with failure. People are so afraid of the consequences that they don't adequately explore innovative approaches to problems. In a lot of companies, even the word *risk* itself can raise people's blood pressure. I've worked with many leaders in financial services and other industries that have extensive compliance challenges, and when they hear that word, you can almost see them sweat. They want nothing to do with it. Instead, they opt for simply meeting expectations. That's setting the bar pretty low. In our research, 97 percent of people say that they're comfortable taking risks, but only 55 percent of those people are viewed by others as actually taking risks at work.

This is a major problem. I'm not talking about doing anything illegal, and I'm not pushing for "creative accounting." I'm talking about taking risks while creating ideas. There will be plenty of opportunity later on to filter out the things that won't work because of regulations, cost, timing, or other real-life restrictions. But in the initial idea-generating phase, everything should be on the table. What's the worst thing that could happen? Someone won't like your idea? Or it might not be the silver bullet that doubles revenues? So what?

The greatest obstacle to taking risks while generating ideas is our natural tendency to link our egos with our ideas. If people don't like my idea, I'll lose their respect. Or it means they hate me as a person. With practice, the inspired individual can separate ego from idea and recognize that most ideas don't belong to one person anyway. Great ideas are born out of collective conversations. And that conversation will never start—or it won't stretch far enough—if everyone is too afraid to throw out an idea.

Sometimes risk-taking can really get the momentum started. Here's a way to bring it to life: you're sitting around with your friends or family on a Friday night. It's been a long week, and everyone is tired. No one wants to cook, but you don't feel like going out either. So you decide to have some food delivered. You ask the group, "What kind of food should we order?"

There is brief murmuring. No one cares. All you hear is "Whatever you want" or "I am open for anything." You pass the issue back and forth across the room while everyone remains determinedly undecided and complacent. Finally you suggest, "What about Chinese?"

Now everyone has an opinion. "Too heavy." "No, I had Chinese last night." "We always order Chinese. Let's try something else." But if you hadn't thrown out Chinese food as a possibility, the conversation would never have started. So don't be afraid to be the one to toss out the first idea, make the first suggestion, and challenge others to respond.

And don't take it personally if they want to order something else.

Taking risk is never comfortable, but it is at the heart of some of the world's greatest moments, innovations, businesses, and achievements. Lead by example by showing others around

Rewarding Risk

Desperation is often the mother of innovation.

In 1995, a large client of ours — Park Avenue, Fortune 100, flush with cash — was ninety days late with our payment, and I was forty-eight hours from having to tell my team that no one would get a paycheck that month. Or worse.

We'd sent letters. We'd sent presents. We'd left voice mails. We'd even had our lawyers call (gently). And we'd gotten nothing. One of my teammates took Gekko, my golden retriever, around the block to clear her head and try to think of a solution. After ten minutes, she burst through the door and announced, "We thought it through, and I think Gekko and I are on to something." Minutes later, to my own disbelief, we had faxed a huge international conglomerate a note from my dog.

Dear Laura,

My name is Gekko, and I'm Andy's 43 pound golden retriever mix. I come to Play every day and am the corporate canine. My title is top dog.

I've been going home with Andy in the evening to an empty dog bowl, and I don't know if it has anything to do with accounts receivables at Play. If it does, I would appreciate any consideration.

I look forward to meeting you when you come visit the Stefanovichs' new row house in Richmond. I'll show you my small, but fun, backyard.

Thanks,
Gekko

The next day, Jason, our UPS guy (and who, seventeen years later, is still our UPS guy) delivered an overnight package with a check for $93,000 and a dog biscuit.

Was what we did risky? No question about it. But sending the Gekko fax took the discussion out of accounts payable and

> made it about people. And once that happened, our relationship blossomed. Since then, we've done more than $15 million in business with that client. And it's always paid its bills. But more than that, it was the transparency we exhibited that led to an amazing relationship.

you that you aren't afraid to speak your mind and take risks when creating ideas. The ripple effect will astonish you.

Try Some Stand-Up

Over the years, I've developed a quick and elegant way to highlight the way that fear of failure impedes our ability to create. Try out this script:

Now let's have some laughs. You have two minutes to create a one-minute stand-up comedy routine. Come up with something—keep it short—that you can do or say that is going to make everyone in this room laugh. You can stand on your head, tell a joke, or do an impression—whatever it takes. You have a few minutes, and then we'll share. The clock starts now. Go.

Give them a few minutes to stew in this knowledge. Notice who looks most upset or fearful. Right before choosing the first people to present their routines, ask the group,

How you are you all feeling?

Whether or not they admit it, most will be panicked. Quickly choose three to five people and ask them to come up to the front of the room. Notice the reactions of everyone who isn't being chosen. Let the group at the front of the room stand there for a little bit, as you notice who looks nervous and who looks confident. Say,

Okay, so how are you all feeling now? I noticed the strategies for not being picked . . . first there was the avoidance of eye contact, and shrinking in seats to become invisible. Then the bluff: bold staring and attentiveness to fake me out.

Now ask each person you've chosen,

How do you feel? Why? What are you afraid of, nervous about?

Reactions will range from "Yeah, I'm ready" to "I'm terrified" to "I have nothing to share." There will likely be a spectrum of answers, and you might have to seed their responses to get to the conclusion that it is very nerve-wracking to be given such an assignment. Next ask,

What about the rest of you in the audience? How do you feel? Why? What are you afraid of, nervous about?

Responses will likely be "relieved" or "glad it's not me up there." Then change the equation:

Here's the twist. I'm not going to ask any of you to go with it. You may sit down.

As the folks at the front of the room return to their seats, there will likely be groans and sighs of relief throughout the room. Now, explain the purpose of the experience:

Isn't this situation exactly the same as when we are asked to share our ideas? The fear that someone might not like them or that they may not provide the ultimate solution sometimes prevents us from sharing. That's why we need to skin our knees. If we don't risk failure, we can't grow. And often the actual risks of failure are far less than what we perceive them to be.

Really do try it out when you have the chance. It's a great—and slightly traumatic—way to bring to life the challenges that all people face when creating ideas. By encouraging your team to risk failure, to skin their knees, you help develop a more innovative and creative mindset throughout the organization.

Think About Your Risk-Taking Mindset

How does your attitude toward risk-taking shape your approach to innovation? Explore that idea by asking yourself these questions:

- When was the last time you did or said something out of character?
- Who is a source of energy and inspiration for you at work? Why?
- What is the role of practicality in the creative process? What is the role of blue-sky thinking?
- What are the boundaries or guardrails of your creative process? (Boundaries you can push, and guardrails to guide your thinking.)
- What kills creativity?
- Do you say what's on your mind—what's *really* on your mind?
- What was a professional risk you took recently? What made it risky?
- How do you challenge yourself on a daily basis?
- If you lost your job tomorrow, what would you do?
- When is a mistake insurmountable?

Find Your Passion

No matter what skills or knowledge we have, we can't succeed personally or professionally without passion—the intense enthusiasm we have for an activity that drives us to reach new levels. Gallup polls regularly find that 50 to 60 percent of the U.S. working population is not engaged while at work.[7] Many of us naturally create a barrier between what we love to do and what we're paid to do. We experience subtle cues every day that encourage us to avoid the connection between our personal passions and our professional duties.

As a leader, you need to develop opportunities that allow your team to share and apply their personal passions to their work goals. A shift in mindset can change the unfortunate separation between the two. By tapping into the enthusiasm of team members' outside-of-work passions, you can align their talents and energy with business goals and help them perform to their full potential.

Put Passion into Action

Let me share with you a method that I often use with participants in our creative programs; I call it Passion in Action. The following is an example from a session I conducted with a clothing manufacturer that was working to sell multiple brands to a single retailer. The group was having trouble working together to achieve better sales penetration into a specific retail customer. The individual brands often worked in silos with the retailer rather than as a manufacturer across brands.

I started by asking the participants to pair off with a partner and share with each other a single passion—something that he or she has a strong desire and excitement to pursue. Whenever I use this method, the level of energy in the room is contagious, going up about five notches. People love to talk about—and, more important, learn about—what makes themselves and others excited. This group was no exception.

One person talked about her passion for sailing, something she learned from a boyfriend long ago during summers spent in the Gulf of Mexico. Another talked about cooking, a skill she picked up during college as a sous-chef to help her pay tuition. Yet another shared his passion for carpentry, a skill he learned as a child in his grandfather's backyard workshop. One member of the group had been an amateur ballet dancer, studying ballet throughout college. It was a passion she still pursued many years later as an instructor's assistant with a community dance company.

After a moment of sharing, I asked the pairs to deconstruct their passion, breaking it down into actions or aspects they particularly enjoyed about their passion. On giant sheets of butcher paper taped to the wall, they wrote out the actions, behaviors, and aspects of their passion. Across the ballet dancer's sheet was neatly drawn the following list (details were elaborated on during the group discussion):

- **It takes discipline and practice**. The discipline of rehearsal gave this participant the technical skill she used to express herself artistically. The rehearsals helped her set achievable goals and work toward mastering those goals. Whether learning a new move or perfecting a particular position, through the discipline of practice, each session helped her build her passion.

- **It takes trust**. In one of the most memorable moments in this exercise, the participant talked about the level of trust she had for her partner during "lifts." She knew that if her partner was going to drop her, he would sacrifice himself to break her fall. This level of trust was built over time and gave her the confidence to perform elaborate lifts with focus and determination.

- **It's organic.** For her, the ability to communicate artistically through technical dance moves was appealing. She was able to "express the emotion of her heart through the technical moves of her body." The technical moves, when combined, allowed her to express complex emotions like love and sorrow through dance.
- **It is a celebration of achievement.** Each time a new move was perfected, she and her partner felt a new level of pride and achievement. There were small celebrations throughout the process between her and her partner. These small celebrations culminated in the final performance, with the applause and recognition of the audience. For her, there were levels of achievement in ballet that allowed for celebration throughout the process of learning that were just as important as the final performance.

After the pairs captured their lists, I reconvened the group and had each pair share their passion and passion in action with the larger team. When the ballet dancer shared her passion of dance and its components, the group discussed how to incorporate aspects of her passion into their work goal:

- **It takes discipline and practice.** The group committed to working together to develop new customer selling techniques—even rehearsing those techniques in role-playing sessions with one another. They did not develop the solution overnight, but instead worked together to develop the smaller skills they needed to sell their product line to larger retail customers.
- **It takes trust.** By committing to work as a team rather than in silos, the group built trust over time. Eventually, the group was able to meet all sales goals together by creating a holistic apparel solution for the retailer.

- **It is a celebration of achievement**. The group committed to celebrating their achievements together, both the development achievements they set for themselves in preparation of the final pitch and the increased sales the group achieved after the pitch.

If you can break down personal passions into their component parts, you'll be able to make the same kinds of connections to the work you and your team do every day. In the process, you'll help stoke those personal passions and put them to work for you, your team, and your organization.

Integrate Your Passions into Every Area of Your Life

Your passion is your bedrock. You need to dig down and find it, connect with it, and build up from there. Stew Friedman is a Wharton professor, author, and a major source of inspiration for my thinking about incorporating my passions into my life and work. In his book *Total Leadership: Be a Better Leader, Have a Richer Life,* he teaches ways to bring the four domains of life—yourself, your work, your community, and your family—together. Friedman doesn't believe in "work-life balance." Instead, he says that we need to integrate all the domains of our life so that each one feeds the others. "You can have mutual gains among the domains," he told me recently, "but the integration is the key for tapping into what truly inspires people—giving people the freedom to pursue the things that matter to them. Sometimes it doesn't directly involve your work in obvious ways, so you need to be creative about that, but with concerted effort you will see big returns in all four domains."[8]

Every one of us has a passion, with unique memories, emotions, and desires associated with that passion. It is a very personal and important source of energy and direction. Too often, our passions are completely disconnected from our jobs. But it doesn't have to be that way. Unleashing your own passion in your life and your work—or at a minimum, using it to fuel your creative process—is an important step in developing an inspired, creative mindset.

Want to see a real-life example of someone who followed her personal passion and integrated it seamlessly into her work? Next time you're in New York, give yourself the gift of stopping into a Vosges Haut-Chocolat boutique. Vosges is owned by Katrina Markoff, who graduated from the prestigious Le Cordon Bleu culinary school in Paris with a specialty in making pastries and other treats. Besides cooking, Markoff's passion is experiencing other cultures. And she's combined the two to build a highly successful business.

Instead of going straight to one of the world's top restaurants as most of her classmates did, Markoff spent eight months traveling the world, interning at different restaurants, trying to find inspiration for new and exotic flavor combinations. She also found inspiration in architecture, religion, and rituals. Then she began creating chocolate. Her experiences in following her passion have resulted in unexpected and inspired flavor combinations that read like an explorer's travel journal: ginger, wasabi, black sesame seeds, and dark chocolate; Tibetan goji berries, pink Himalayan salt, and deep milk chocolate; Oaxacan guajillo and pasilla chillies with Tanzanian bittersweet chocolate; Kalamata olives and Venezuelan white chocolate. The list goes on and on. And Markoff is always hunting for new combinations.

When Markoff applied her passion for the world's diverse cultures to her work—sweets—she found a rewarding life and a strategic edge. What started as a batch of exotic truffles has become multiple product lines, retail stores, and a global mission. Vosges uses renewable energy, works with environmental groups and grassroots community organizations, and tries to bridge cultural barriers. All with chocolate. Markoff's passion shines through in the Vosges mission statement: "If we can embrace the idea of trying something new such as the perplexing oddity of curry and chocolate, we just may come one step closer to bringing peace to the world through chocolate. One Love, One Chocolate."[9]

Distill Essence down to Oneword

The simplest way to connect with your passion and those of others is Oneword. Ask yourself, "If I could choose just one word that completely embodies me, what would it be?"

As a first try, many people say "Fun" or "Family." But if you think about it long enough, you'll probably find something a lot less generic. What's a more unique word that represents your personal essence or your "way"? What makes you different? What gets you excited and engaged? Often that word is your passion.

I frequently use Oneword with large groups of leaders as a kind of catalyst for jump-starting communication. Instead of "Hi, I am Joe Smith, senior vice president of sales and marketing for the plastics division," a conversation might start with, "Hi, I am Joe Smith, and my Oneword is Mountaineer."

More often than not, once people start talking about their Oneword, I have a hard time getting them to stop. Once people connect with their passions and share them with others, they unleash untapped potential energy. Channeling that energy toward their professional dreams and their day-to-day duties takes practice, but can yield big business results.

Oneword is a very powerful concept, and I'd love to take complete credit for having come up with it. But the truth is that the spark came from my mother-in-law. One morning, over Cheerios and fresh OJ, she leaned over and said, "In all of our conversations since we met, I still haven't figured out what is at your very core. What is the one word that completely embodies you?" That simple question has gone on to change the way I work.

That we've incorporated something my mother-in-law said into the way we run our business is yet another proof that inspiration for creating and innovating isn't the result of secret formulas, complicated algorithms, and black boxes. It is, in many ways, common sense unleashed.

Develop "Business Crushes"

I seek out and surround myself with people who are passionate. A lot of them work with me; others are mentors and tremendous sources of inspiration. I call them "business crushes," and I have hundreds—you've read about some of them in this book, but there are many, many more (and you know who you are).

Business crushes hit you just like their more amorous counterparts you experienced when you were thirteen years old. You get butterflies in your stomach. You make special trips out of your way just to catch a glimpse. You try to run into them, lingering a little in the hallway when you see them coming. You trip over your words because they are so special, so interested and interesting. You want to learn from them and get to know them. Your heart flutters when you see their name

Flying Kibble

Gilles Barathier has two great passions—machines and making things better. Fortunately for him, he is in charge of increasing efficiency at a dog and cat food factory in St. Denis de l'Hôtel, France, for Mars Incorporated. (Mars makes more than just candy.)

When the funnels that fill the pet food bags were regularly clogging, Gilles went to work seeking a solution, but not within the environment of the plant or his industry, or even with his colleagues. He sought inspiration from his former life as an aviation mechanic, and found his answer in his passion for the physics of helicopter flight. The vortex effect created by helicopter rotors inspired a new approach that Gilles applied to the bag-filling process.

Instead of just pouring the food into the top of the funnel and hoping it wouldn't clog on its way into the bag, Gilles created a helicopter-like dynamic by blasting a thin stream of air inside the cone. The resulting circulation of air enabled the bits of food to swirl down the funnel into the bags more consistently than before. This technique not only solved the clogging problem but increased the overall speed of the factory line.

At first glance, the physics of helicopter flight and kibble don't seem related, but Gilles followed his passion for flight and found an unlikely innovation.[10]

THINK

on an Outlook invite. Why? Because business crushes unleash your passions. They allow you to be the most of yourself. Your truest You. They are the people who inspire you because they are people in business, not just businesspeople.

I always take something away from a conversation with a business crush that makes me a better Me in every area of my life—personal, professional, and otherwise.

Who are your business crushes? I'm sure you have a few. If so, drop them a line every once in a while to let them know how much they inspire you. Share your ideas. Collaborate and draw inspiration from them. I've mentioned a few in my acknowledgments—that's how important they are.

Think About Your Personal and Professional Passions

Thinking about how passion plays out in your life will make it a lot easier for you to connect the most important characteristics of your personal passions to your work. Go ahead, give it a try. Start by asking yourself these questions:

- What is your passion?
- What's your passion in action?
- How can you incorporate more of those elements into your work 24/7/365?
- How similar is your "work persona" to your "home persona"?
- What gives you energy on a daily basis?
- What do you always make time for because you enjoy it?
- How well do you know your coworkers?
- What's one thing you'd like to accomplish as a retired person?
- What would your coworkers be surprised to learn about you?
- What would you like to do at work that is not technically part of your job description?
- At work, are you black and white, grey, or Technicolor?
- Do you love what you do? Why or why not?
- What does work-life integration mean to you?

Establish Confusion Tolerance: Challenge Assumptions and Embrace Ambiguity

How much time do you give yourself to generate new ideas? In general, people are uncomfortable with the ambiguity of not having an immediate idea or solution to a situation. To end this discomfort, we generate a quick idea and then apply it. Typically, these ideas are "low-hanging fruit"—rehashed or recycled bits of ideas that are neither new nor novel, as in, "If it worked last quarter, it will work again this quarter—no need to reinvent the wheel." As a creative catalyst, you need to give your team permission to generate and explore several new ideas before choosing a solution. I call this *confusion tolerance.*

Quit Rushing and Set Aside Time to Find Options

My arrival into Chennai, India, in 2007 brought on serious culture shock. I lost track of the number of connecting flights, and by the time the plane touched down, I was jet-lagged out of my mind. Kannon, the driver from the hotel, met my teammate Ben Armbruster and me at the airport, and we sped off toward the center of the city. It was a harrowing ride. As Kannon wove in and out of traffic—seemingly oblivious to lanes or oncoming traffic—he never slowed down. Not even for red lights.

When we finally got through the downtown traffic and I regained the ability to speak, I asked Kannon about the red lights. He answered quickly, his eyes never leaving the road, "Those are not good lights, sir. I stop at the important lights."

Once we were delivered safely to the hotel, we checked in and then immediately set off for a walk. As scary as it was to be in a speeding car, it didn't take us long to realize that being out of one was even worse. It was a scene of complete chaos. Auto-rickshaws, buses, cars, and motorcycles all competed for space. Small children and dogs shot out from alleys. Cows, elaborately decorated for the harvest festival of Pongal, munched sugarcane at every corner and wandered in the roadway. The abundance of street vendors and overgrown trees forced pedestrians from the sidewalk into traffic. One auto-rickshaw came so close to me that I could smell the driver's sweat. And of course, no one paid any attention to the stoplight where we were waiting to cross. Red. Green. Red. Green. Nothing changed but the color of the light.

The longer we waited, the more determined we were to cross the street and explore the neighborhood. Every few minutes one of us would step off the curb, only to be pulled back by the other. Finally, we saw a small gap between two buses and took off sprinting. We barely made it. In Chennai, a simple thing like crossing the street was an extreme sport. I was amazed that the roadway wasn't littered with broken bodies.

We walked for a block or two before the stifling heat, dehydration, and exhaustion hit us both, and we turned around. Taking a deep breath, we bolted across the street, risking our lives for a hot shower and a soft bed.

The next day, I asked Kannon whether there were a lot of accidents involving pedestrians. "Oh no, sir," he replied. "It is very safe." I told him about our street-crossing adventure and how we'd nearly been killed. Twice. He flashed a huge grin and laughed. "You silly Americans," he said. "You don't run through traffic in Chennai. You walk. That way the drivers can gauge your speed and direction. They will go around you. They don't want to hit you. But if you run ... well ... then they might just hit you."

Later on that day, my teammate and I decided to test Kannon's advice. As you can imagine, it took a phenomenal leap of faith, completely contrary to our saner instincts. The roiling sea of flatbed trucks, motorcycles, limos, and rickshaws simply parted as we tentatively—but slowly—walked to the other side of the boulevard.

I'm telling you this story for a number of reasons. First, it's got great visuals and a little tension, which are just fun. Second, it's a great analogy to what's happening with leaders today. Basically, we're trained to look for the solution that makes the most sense and run toward it—hard. Finally, this story shows the importance of shifting your mindset and not allowing yourself to get locked into one "solution." Business leaders rarely challenge their assumptions or spend much time exploring alternatives—especially seemingly counterintuitive

Go Find It

If I gave you the order to "Go find it," what would you do? It's a pretty ambiguous directive, but I had a good look at this exercise in embracing ambiguity when working with an associate from a major beverage company. On one occasion, he had about two hundred people relocate to the lawn outside the Ritz-Carlton Hotel; he said he'd finally found the weather he'd been looking for, and wanted us to have it as well. Another time, he walked out of a meeting and came back half an hour later with . . . a client. He'd found someone who fit the company's target demographic and asked him to join us. This kind and interesting man spent two hours with our brand group and even had lunch with us. For an up-close experience with exploring possibilities and embracing ambiguity, go find it—find the weather, a client, or whatever hits you.

THINK

ones. But if you want to get across the street in Chennai, India, or you want to get beyond the obvious sources of innovation and start thinking differently, you're going to have to take that first step. It's not going to be easy—although creating a mindset that's conducive to inspiration makes it a hell of a lot easier—and it's going to take a bit of faith.

Practice Confusion Tolerance

I strive to hire people who are smart and talented, and we think it's never too soon to start changing the world. So when Ben Armbruster and Barry Saunders (both of whom you've met in earlier stories) first joined Play, I introduced them to the other members of the team, told them about a few great lunch spots, and then put them to work. "We need to reinvent a conference for some marketing professionals at a Fortune 10 company," I said. "Take ninety minutes and generate five hundred ideas."

Ben and Barry were a little stunned, and pressed me with questions: "How many people are at the conference?" "What kind of company is it?" "What are their market dynamics?" "What is the content of the conference?" "What outcomes are they looking for?"

But I gave them no more instructions. "You've both been to plenty of conferences, so you know how they are. *Reinvent it!* You've only got eighty-eight minutes left."

Ben and Barry set off to a local coffee shop in Richmond and started to create a large volume of ideas. The first one hundred or so were exactly what you'd expect from two guys on their first day, trying to find the perfect solution. Have it at a different kind of venue. Seat people in a big circle. Have "out there" speakers. Have leather-bound journals and nice pens instead of hotel notepads and pens...

But as they pushed into the four hundreds, the ideas took on a different quality. The entire session will take place on a train. It should be a circus with elephants. Participants should learn to man actual nuclear submarines and engage in a war game. There should be no clothing allowed. They should turn the entire conference into a twenty-four-hour news channel, and no one would sleep. The CEO should drive up and down the East Coast in a stretch limousine and pick up each participant.

This was Ben and Barry's first experience with our process. Once they removed the filter of "the perfect solution," they found themselves in completely new—and far more creative—territory. Of course about 450 of the ideas didn't make it into reality, but the one about the CEO and the limousine turned into an idea our client loved. Participants needed to understand that their senior managers cared about their attending the conference. They were investing in their professional development.

So instead of having the senior leaders issue a standard e-mail or Outlook invite, we asked them to write a personal note, expressing the importance of growing and learning at the conference. And the moral of this story is that the participants did feel more engaged while they attended the conference. They shared what they learned with their teams back at the office and used those opportunities to help develop others who weren't at the conference. I don't think we would ever have ended up with that idea if Ben and Barry hadn't gotten beyond the need to find a quick—and obvious—solution.

We used the same approach when a U.S. media giant brought us in to help facilitate the integration of three different sales divisions. The organizations weren't getting along well; they were communicating poorly and constantly bickering over limited budgets. The company's top management recognized that they needed a new way of working together and a different level of intimacy.

Our team didn't jump to a fast solution. Instead, we generated more than three hundred ideas and decided to try a variation on number 208: "Have the conference in a giant bed so people get to know each other differently." To put the idea into action, we brought dozens of beds into a hotel ballroom and had people from each division participate in the meetings from the cozy settings. Boy, did they get to know each other well—and going forward, the different teams started working together more effectively. They had a shared moment of inspiration that forced them to reevaluate the ways that they behave and interact.

As we've just seen, the simplest way to increase your confusion tolerance is to change the way you approach idea generation. Instead of going into it with the specific goal of finding one or two ideas that will drive growth or improve performance, come up with fifty. Or a hundred. And don't stop till you finish the whole list—even if you come up with an idea at number 27 that you think is a winner.

Alternatively, if the prospect of generating a specific number of ideas is too daunting, try setting aside a specific amount of time, say thirty minutes. Or even ten. Set a timer and don't stop until time runs out, no matter how many great ideas you're coming up with. In the beginning, your search for ideas is all about quantity over quality. You can apply whatever filters you want to evaluate the list later on. If you stop when you think you've come up with a winner, you'll never get to the point of stretching yourself. So work with me here and trust the process.

Generating ideas also is a team sport, and your team's success depends on finding the right balance among members' confusion tolerance. Everyone has a different level of tolerance. Sure, you can move the needle a little one way or the other, but it's important that you know where you and your team members are on the spectrum. Are you a divergent thinker who generates possibilities? A convergent thinker who has a knack for honing in on the best ideas and making them real? A blend? Once you know where you are, find others who balance you.

Modern business thrives on speed—Faster. Sooner. Cheaper.—and we're rewarded for delivering solutions as

There Are No Absolutes

Almost ten years ago, I was standing in Trondheim, Norway, with David Storkholm of KaosPilot International, the Denmark-based business design school. It was a beautiful sunny day. We were standing along the waterfront, reflecting on the great experience we just had talking about innovation with a team of Staat Oil executives, when I felt a large liquid splat on the bill of my baseball hat. Fearing that I had been targeted by a seabird, I cautiously examined my hat and found that it was just a raindrop. A very big drop. Soon we were being hit by dozens of golf-ball-size drops despite the apparent lack of clouds in the sky. I was perplexed. Storkholm said, "Andy, I would expect more from you. There are no absolutes." He explained to me that the clouds were so high that we couldn't see them, that this rain was traveling through the blue sky to hit us. I am no meteorologist, but this moment struck me in a powerful way. There are no absolutes. Rain with a clear sky.[11]

THINK

quickly as possible. But if you want a creative mindset, you'll have to take a big step back, put your preconceived notions aside, quit looking for a quick or easy solution, and start considering a lot more options.

Okay, your turn. What are one hundred ideas for your business? Seriously, can you list them?

Stop Looking for Solutions

During one of my first (and always inspirational) visits to Denmark to spend a week collaborating with the folks at KaosPilot International—a passionate force for creative thinking—my colleague Courtney and I set aside a day at the end of our trip to seek out inspiration. We asked the KaosPilots for a suggestion; without a second's hesitation, they said, "Henning. You've got to talk to Henning," and they pointed us in the direction of the Danish Technical Institute.

When we arrived at the institute, we were greeted by Henning Sejer Jakobsen, an exuberant gentleman who looked exactly like Doc from the movie *Back to the Future*—wild hair, wide eyes, white lab coat, and all. "Are you the Americans interested in creativity?" he asked. Before we could answer, he was off, and we found ourselves racing to keep up with him as he toured us through a maze of startling innovations. Chairs suspended from the ceiling and a table made entirely of toothpicks. Posters on the wall with discussions of creativity in dozens of languages. Crazy stuff.

He left us in his stuffy, eight-by-eight-foot office to wait for about forty minutes—talk about testing our confusion tolerance—and then burst back in the room. We were already perplexed, but even more so when Henning stopped in the

Remind Yourself That You Don't Have All the Answers

How many executives blow into a meeting, offer a directive, and blow out again just as quickly? How many ask for your ideas but then cut you off halfway through your first sentence to tell you about their predetermined point of view? How many think their ideas, and only their ideas, are the only ones that matter? The answer to all three questions is, "Too many."

One CEO friend of mine takes the opposite tack. He firmly believes that any idea, at any time, thought up by anyone can change the course of the future. So he spends a lot of time listening to others. He carries a small card in his pocket that reads, "They may be right." And he holds it in his hand as he listens. It makes his conversations equal, true, and authentic, and rich with results.

THINK

middle of a sentence and announced, "If anyone in a creative session of mine offers me a solution quickly, I throw them out!" "Why?" we asked. His reply crystallized for us the importance of confusion tolerance: "What I look for first is thoughts, which lead to ideas, which then lead to solutions." He explained that creativity is about creating possibilities, about exploring multiple sources of inspiration, not solutions. Focusing on solutions too early kills the process.[12]

Avoid the High Cost of Unchallenged Assumptions

Kishore Biyani didn't set out to spend tens of thousands of dollars retrofitting each of his brand-new Big Bazaar and Food Bazaar grocery stores in India. All he was trying to do was enhance the shopping experience for his part of the world by giving customers what he thought they wanted. What better way to do that than to introduce the modern model for convenience and choice to India?

Kishore's stores were full of modern amenities. They had nice wide aisles, bright lights, and well-ordered shelves. They were air-conditioned, clean, calm, and organized. In fact, each store looked very much like a Walmart, which was created thousands of miles away by one of Biyani's heroes, Sam Walton.

Inspired by Walton's model, Biyani opened his own chain of megastores in India, but he was surprised by his customers' initial reactions. They walked in, looked around, and walked right back out. Why? It wasn't for lack of merchandise—there was everything on his shelves that customers would find in the local market, except that the shelves were neater and cleaner, and the items were easier to find and buy quickly. How could the same items in a better environment not be attractive?

Then he realized that he'd built his business model on an assumption that turned out to be completely false—that the Western, Walmart model would succeed for Indian retail. His customers didn't want modern and more efficient; they wanted what was familiar. Biyani's potential customers didn't even know how to shop in the environment he had created for them. It was too foreign, too clean, too organized. Most of the customers were used to the crowded, bustling, chaotic vibe of Indian markets. In that context, shopping means hunting, haggling, stooping, rooting through baskets, and edging out other shoppers for the best items. Pretty much the same thing you see in American department stores toward the end of a big sale.

Biyani had created great ideas, but for the wrong objective. He couldn't create a successful retail model for his customers by recreating the American model. Once he realized his error, he quickly set out to make changes in the stores and capitalize on what his shoppers expected (even if that meant doing things that seemed counterintuitive). He generated hustle and crowding by kinking the aisles and making them narrow at points, so that shopping carts and people would form bottlenecks. He turned off the air-conditioning in some stores. He resisted sanitizing the displays. If customers benefited from the thrill of the find, he would cover good produce with bad. If being able to feel the quality of beans was equated with freshness, he would remove them from their packages. If chaos equals bargains, he would orchestrate chaos. He hired more employees and started using megaphones to announce sales in the moment, in local languages. If food was spilled, he'd leave it on the floor awhile instead of cleaning it right up. If a light bulb went out, so be it.

Those changes resonated with consumers, and before long, his Big Bazaar annual sales were so popular that police had to come quell a potential riot. In challenging his initial assumption to follow Sam Walton's model, Biyani found the real opportunity: to blend cultural shopping habits into a modern retail environment that delivers front-of-house familiarity with back-of-house efficiency and improved margins.[13]

Do unchallenged assumptions misdirect your creative thinking? What kinds of assumptions do you bring with you into your decision-making process? If you aren't comfortable challenging your assumptions, you may find yourself pursuing all the wrong possibilities or arriving at solutions that are a terrible fit for the situation at hand.

Think About Your Ability to Embrace Confusion Tolerance

How would you answer these questions? Take a few minutes.

- Go find it. (How would you handle this directive?)
- Which word do you prefer: *ideas, possibilities,* or *solutions*?
- Do you like deciding or creating?
- Imagine living abroad for a year. Where would you live and why?
- How many ideas do you have daily?
- Think of your last vacation. How structured was your itinerary?
- When you go shopping, do you prefer to browse or buy?
- What is the role of decision making in the creative process?
- When you go for a walk, do you plan the route first?
- Do you prefer working alone or in a group?

Skull a Day

I have not experienced a more ideal expression of these Mindset disciplines than when working with graphic artist and friend Noah Scalin.

Noah accepted a challenge: to create an artistic interpretation of a skull in a new medium every day for 365 days. Every day, Noah created a different design in a different medium—from soap to the bottom of a Converse shoe—and posted the results on his blog.[14] His challenge captures our four tenets of creativity:

1. *Change your perspective:* Working with friends and colleagues in different media forced Noah to explore, learn, and apply new perspectives to his work. How often do you bring divergent perspectives to bear on your project or objective?
2. *Skin your knees:* Trying new media gave Noah permission to experiment and take risks. How often do you give yourself

permission to approach a challenge through an unfamiliar and unproven method?

3. *Find your passion:* Spending four hours a day working on a project fueled Noah's affection for art, learning, and creating. How often do you apply a personal passion to your objectives?

4. *Establish confusion tolerance:* Each day, Noah approached his challenge with only two certainties: (1) he had only twenty-four hours to create something new; (2) he would be working in a medium in which he did not have deep expertise (for example, baking bread). How often do you let your innovation become paralyzed with analysis rather than trusting a process and creating from scratch?

As you think about Noah Scalin's project (see note 14), consider his thoughts on creativity and the discipline of inspiration. Ask yourself these questions to gauge your creative mindset:

- Are you fully aware of all the inspiration around you that might lead to a business solution?
- What can you do each and every day to be more creative and find ideas for your unique challenges?
- What's the worst that can happen if one of your ideas isn't the ultimate solution?
- What are you passionate about creating? Value? Ideas? Relationships? What else?

Okay, Now You Try . . .

Throughout this chapter, I've asked you to think about questions related to your (and your team's) mindset in terms of inspiration, creativity, and innovation. Before we move on to the next M, Mechanisms, take a minute to think about your mindset as a whole, then ask yourself these questions:

- How many minutes a day do you set aside to come up with possibilities instead of solutions?
- Do your people look for *the* answer or form their top one hundred ideas on any given objective?
- When is the last time you sought out tangential and abstract inspiration?
- Do people have to preface questions with the statement "OK. Now for the dumb question . . ."?

CHAPTER 3

Mechanisms

Mechanisms are the tools and processes that bring your creativity and innovation to life.

Having read the previous two chapters, you've already begun developing the mood and mindset that are most conducive to driving inspiration. So now let's talk about how to translate all that inspiration into ideas. The way we're going to do that is by using *mechanisms*.

In this chapter, you're going to learn to use tools and processes, no doubt about it. But when I use the word "mechanisms," I'm not speaking only in that traditional sense. I have long believed that some of the most powerful tools and techniques are not actually tools and techniques at all. They're much more of a frame of reference, a state of mind, a philosophy. With time and practice, mastering philosophical mechanisms and certain ways of thinking will help you drive innovation and creativity.

Transforming innovation into ideas involves four steps:

1. Build a context in which you can create.
2. Generate ideas.
3. Filter your ideas.
4. Create a blueprint that will help you implement the best ideas.

Before we dive into these four steps, let's stop to take a closer look at the relationship between innovation and ideas.

Put Ideas in Their Place

To begin, it's important that we all agree on what, exactly, the word *idea* means. For our purposes, think of ideas as simple statements that express an objective and a means for accomplishing it:

"In order to _____, we will _____."

For example:

In order to increase employee retention, we will increase engagement.

In order to de-position a competitor, we will create a new business model.

In order to increase market share, we will introduce new products.

Like I said—a simple statement. But be careful. Statements like "It will be really cool if we can open a second location" and "We're going to knock our competitors out of the market" are *not* ideas. They're goals. And although goals are nice, they aren't actionable. Ideas are. Your idea statement needs to say what action you will take and why you will take it.

Use Ideas and Innovations of Every Size

One of the keys to understanding innovation is that it comes in many sizes. Innovation is often associated with big game-changing ideas like the iPod or hybrid vehicles, but some innovations can be small. And many small innovations can add up to a lot of growth and change. Innovations come in a variety of packages, but here are the three basic flavors:

- **Incremental.** These are the types of small changes that might make you say, "Why haven't we always been doing that?" or "Why didn't I think of that?" Here's an example: Remember when air fresheners came in just one form and one scent—the classic Lysol clinical smell? Someone eventually thought to add new scents like "Mountain Breeze" and "Crisp Linen." That slight twist on an existing product grew the overall market. Same product, just a different color, scent, or size. Incremental innovation often requires little investment of resources.

- **Breakthrough.** These innovations create a distinct shift in a product, service, or process while adding value. They often require more research, development, and investment. For example, some researcher or product engineer noticed that spray air-freshener scents dissipate quickly, and wondered, "What if the scent could be delivered continually?" Thus, the plug-in air freshener was born, a product that includes multiple ideas for innovation—electricity, fans, hands-free, and continual deodorizing. Breakthrough innovations stretch us and might make us a little uncomfortable, but they're still relatively close to our core businesses.

- **Transformational.** Transformational innovations revolutionize an organization or create a paradigm shift in an industry or a market. They might create a new category or a brand-new market. Think iTunes, eBay, or Craigslist. Or the light bulb, the automobile, and nuclear power. Or, to stay with our earlier example, consider technologies that incorporate air-freshening scents directly into floor coverings and clothing. Those technologies have redefined a business that was once a consumer packaged good; now textile manufacturers can be in the air-freshener business, and vice versa. Transformational ideas such as these can seem scary and unachievable when they first come up—they demand time, energy, leadership, and vision—but they can also deliver the greatest value.

When we're talking about ideas for innovation with our clients, we often say things like, "We need one transformational, a couple of breakthroughs, with some incrementals sprinkled around." Your life and your work also will require innovations and ideas of every type and size. Remember that each of these three types of innovation, even the most incremental, can carry tremendous power, and these categories can help you organize your innovation pipeline. Create a blended portfolio with different ideas that have varying degrees of speed to market, resources needed, and potential impact, so that you aren't left behind if a big investment in a transformational idea doesn't pay off.

In this chapter, I am going to walk you through mechanisms for generating ideas; it is important to use them to create ideas in each of the three categories.

One-Degree Difference

Here's an example of how much difference the smallest change can make: teammate Geof Hammond and I were at the Ford Leadership Center in Detroit, and we were having a hard time getting a group of engineers from all over the world to completely grasp the idea—and the importance—of LAMSTAIH. They wanted efficiency and technical improvements, and couldn't understand how inspiration could enhance their creative processes.

As we considered how to connect the audience to the content, Geof and I took a moment to look out the window of the meeting room. It was a few days before Christmas. Overnight, the temperature had dipped to thirty-two degrees, and the whole city was covered in snow. We asked all the engineers to come over to one side of the room, where floor-to-ceiling windows overlooked a pristine white field bordered by snow-capped trees. We asked them about waking up to see the snow, their commutes to the session, and how the snow made them feel. The group shared their thoughts about happiness, anticipation of the upcoming holiday, listening to holiday music in the car, and feeling a sense of potential. Then we asked them to consider a change of one degree. How would everything be different if the temperature had fallen only to thirty-three degrees? They described images of frozen rain, piles of gray slush, and soggy fields. Another rainy commute with the usual inconveniences: wet jeans, soaked shoes, the drone of radio reports about bad traffic and a down economy. The only thing separating idyllic feelings of holiday happiness from visions of headaches, problems, and gloom was one degree—the difference between the temperatures of thirty-two and thirty-three.

Sure, sometimes we have an idea that sparks an innovation that becomes a complete game changer. But most of the time, change is about tweaking things a little bit. Just one degree can make a big difference. What's your one degree? What's your team's one degree? How about your organization's?

THINK

Don't Overlook the Space Between

Finding the best road to innovation often involves scouting an unmarked path in a totally new direction. Some of the strongest ideas might be waiting along the way.

Dove has been in the soap business for a long time. Recently, when it set out to grow sales for its personal care products, the company spent some time looking at more stuff and thinking about it harder. The typical focus for this kind of research falls on the standard "four P's"—product, pricing, placement, and promotion. Dove, branching off in a new direction entirely, asked women of all ages to share their ideas about beauty in general.

The results were stunning, if not unexpected. Of all the women surveyed, only 2 percent described themselves as beautiful. Almost everyone else said that the popular representations of beauty were unattainable. These insights gave Dove the opportunity to reshape the discussion of beauty and also the entire beauty products market. The company started the Dove Campaign for Real Beauty, an advertising campaign that has become a global movement to build self-esteem and shatter unrealistic stereotypes of women's bodies.

Dove drove sales by addressing the context in which its products live—women's notions of beauty—not the products themselves. Its space between turned a "low" marketing challenge (sell more soap) into a "high" one (a grassroots movement to raise women's self-esteem). In the process, Dove landed right in the middle of a marketer's dream: selling more products while enhancing the brand, strengthening relationships with consumers, and changing a cultural conversation. It doesn't get any better than that.[1]

Sometimes finding the space between is actually more tactical. In 2002, a college in Dublin was in crisis. For some reason, its restrooms were a popular place for local drug addicts to shoot up in private. And one day, a heroin addict OD'd and died in the restroom. There was a public outcry about the safety of the student body. Many demanded that something be done to stop the illegal activity. But the college's leaders didn't have a lot of options. They couldn't afford to hire a guard for every restroom in every building. And locking all the bathrooms wouldn't be fair to people who needed to use them for their intended purpose.

Luckily, someone had a bright idea—literally. The college installed inexpensive ultraviolet lights in the restrooms. Under the lights' eerie blue glow, the drug users couldn't see their veins (which appear blue under the skin) and therefore couldn't shoot up. The college leaders found the space between because they took time to explore a narrower issue. Instead of attacking the

Parameters—Set 'em and Forget 'em

We always go into idea generation with some definition of what success looks like. Although we've talked about not being boxed in by preconceived notions, it's very rare that anyone begins a project that is completely undefined: unlimited budget, no clear success criteria, no timeline—just go and create some great innovation. Instead, we usually have concrete direction in terms of timing, resources, and anticipated results.

When you use any of the mechanisms in this chapter, you most likely will come to the process with a budget, timeline, market, brand, or any number of influences. That said, once you know what the parameters are, you need to set 'em and forget 'em. As a rule of thumb, creating against criteria kills exploration. Reserve the evaluation until you have completed idea generation.

THINK

problem at the high level on which it was presented (keeping drug addicts out of public restrooms), the college found a smaller, more practical opportunity and made the restrooms unattractive to drug addicts yet fully functional for the general public.

Dove and the college in Dublin were both successful because they broke down their challenges into their fundamental components—beyond the obvious—to find new opportunities. Several of the mechanisms in this chapter help you do just that.

Build Your Context to Create

Your first step in the process of generating ideas and transforming them into innovation is to build a context for creating—setting the right expectations, so that ideas can flourish and mechanisms are used in the right way. But before we can get into the step-by-step idea-generation mechanisms, we need to understand the context in which we create and the kinds of ideas you will be looking for.

Your context to create is what I like to call the "innovation architecture"—the framework you build within your organization's mood and mindset that will give your creative and innovative ideas the traction they need to thrive. To provide that kind of creative context, your innovation architecture must make use of three approaches:

- Elegant solutions
- The Bigger Big
- Framing

Let's take a look at these in more detail.

Accommodate Elegant Solutions

We all know what solutions are. But *elegant* solutions are something different. Rather than resolve a single problem, elegant solutions have multiple benefits, meaning that they meet the needs of more than one objective. Here's one example:

For many people considering cosmetic surgery, the two biggest obstacles are price and privacy. The procedures are almost never covered by insurance, and patients don't want anyone to know that they have had the work done. Rather than shelling out top dollar and then hiding at home covered in bandages, many people go to South Africa, Costa Rica, or other places where prices are lower and where they can recuperate in relative privacy, while touring lush game parks or relaxing on the beach. Imagine how refreshed and relaxed people seem—and look—when they return from their "rhino and rhinoplasty safaris."

Medical tourism, as it's now called, is an elegant solution because it meets both primary needs—cost and privacy—and offers the added benefit of pampering the patient in a lush setting. The burgeoning industry is a boon to both medicine *and* tourism in many countries.

Elegant solutions have a much bigger, much wider impact than ordinary solutions. And in our research, we've found that companies that actively seek out elegant solutions have a greater propensity for innovation and innovate at a faster rate.

Make Space for the Bigger Big

If elegant solutions are the depth of your creative context, then the Bigger Big is its breadth. Incorporating a Bigger Big mentality—change a country, a society, the world—is a key ingredient in building a creative context that's expansive enough to encompass even the most far-reaching ideas and innovations.

An executive at Google once told me that they have simple, but daunting success criteria for certain project initiatives: "We want Google to be solving problems that affect at least a billion people." Although your specific objective might not have the same reach, challenge yourself and your team to deliver value to as many people as possible. It works for Google, and it can work for you.

Frame Challenges

Your innovation architecture has to provide a very clear and simple framework for developing your ideas into innovations.

I once heard a story that involved an address Bill Gates gave on the radio in India back in the early 1990s, just at the cusp of the technology boom. Gates challenged the Indians to prepare themselves to take full advantage of the coming revolution. He framed his challenge in a simple construct:

1. Buy land.
2. Build a building on it and build airports nearby.
3. Travel the world to find the most brilliant scientists and technologists, and fill the buildings with them.

One of the people listening that day was India's minister of the interior, who took action. Today, India is at the forefront of the tech industry. Are you thinking big enough? And are you giving others a framework for accessing that challenge? There's no question that many ideas are complex. But the individuals and companies that make it a priority to find simpler and more effective ways to access them will win.

Generate More Effective Ideas (with These Eight Mechanisms)

As I mentioned at the opening of the chapter, the mechanisms for idea generation come in many forms; some are techniques, some are processes, and others are team activities. All of the eight mechanisms I've included here are tools that will drive more effective ideas and spark new thinking.

One: Lists, More Lists, and Even More Lists

There are a variety of methods for exploring opportunities, but an essential first step is to create lists of the characteristics that define the issue or objective. This isn't a counting-things-up kind of inventory. What we're doing here is assessing three types of characteristics to find the components with the most opportunities for delivering growth and change:

- **Physical** characteristics are pretty straightforward—obvious descriptive attributes, such as heavy, square, hard, blue, and so on.
- **Functional** characteristics describe less tangible qualities —how something is used and whether people use it the way it was intended or come up with something completely different on their own.
- **Emotional** characteristics are the feelings and emotions people have about whatever it is that they're using (and how they feel if they *can't* have it).

Be sure to put time into creating these lists. The richer and more detailed they are, the greater the chance that you'll come up with breakthrough ideas as you move through the later steps in the mechanism. And don't give in to the temptation to do this in your head. There's something about putting things down on paper that helps get those creative juices flowing. Let me give you a real-life example of lists in action.

Richmond, Virginia, where I live and work, is a city like many others in the United States. Its downtown was once a thriving center of commerce and culture—emphasis on "once"—but a mass exodus to the suburbs in the middle of the twentieth century left downtown with beautiful but decaying buildings, boarded-up storefronts, and very little traffic—pedestrian or otherwise. Richmond is slowly reviving its urban core, but the work is challenging.

The city's chamber of commerce asked me for advice on how to revitalize the downtown area—a huge task that no one had been able to figure out how to accomplish. I met with some members of the chamber, and we began generating ideas.

Because "revitalize downtown" was so overwhelming, the first thing we did was narrow the focus, in the hope of finding something more achievable. We started by making lists, essentially an inventory of Richmond's assets and attributes. Here's what we came up with.

Physical	Office buildings, apartments, buses, parks, the public library, theaters, empty storefronts, hot dog vendors, workers, city employees, police, homeless people, traffic lights, and crosswalks
Functional	Working, begging for change, eating, walking, riding, having lunch, commuting, crossing the street, conversing, buying, and selling
Emotional	Stress, safety, camaraderie, laughter, achievement, respect, sense of history, potential, frustration, and excitement

Creating this multilayered inventory of Richmond's down-town revealed all sorts of interesting opportunities. In fact, there were too many of them. One of the most common comments I hear from people who are dissatisfied with the results from a creative process is that the ideas simply aren't practical. For this reason, it's important to resist the urge to take on a problem that's too large. Creating high-impact, implementable ideas can motivate a group of people to create again, to go back and tackle issues on a grander scale. In situations where engagement and credibility are low, narrowly focusing on one objective can get people's minds (and arms and legs) moving.

So we homed in on a single, workable objective where we could make a short-term impact and build momentum toward our larger goal. The one characteristic of the city that most people seemed drawn to was the public library on Franklin Street. It's an existing public resource that could be the community's cultural center and serve as a focal point for driving more people downtown. By driving traffic to the library downtown, we thought we would be able to attract more shops and vendors who would go where the crowds were.

Once we'd narrowed our focus, we created a similar inventory of the library's assets and attributes.

Physical	Books, librarians, shelves, floor, walls, computers, desks, periodicals, patrons, library cards, drop box
Functional	Reading, checking out books, searching for information, learning, whispering, community posting, membership
Emotional	Introspection, frustration, wonder, loneliness, quiet, excitement, intrigue

There are two main reasons why we spent so much time putting these lists together. First, doing so forced us to find hidden elements that we might otherwise overlook. For example, taking "membership" from the library's functional inventory got us thinking about the various facets of membership: library cards, key tags, overdue notices, "friends of the library" bumper stickers, and so on.

The second purpose of the inventory is to reveal gaps in knowledge among the people who will be creating. In other words, you'll be able to see how literate people are around the topic at hand. If all they see in a library is buildings and books, they don't really know much about libraries. But if they can come up with a list like the one above, they're the kind of people you want on your team.

If you want to dig a little deeper into the list concept, here's a more advanced technique: Remember how we talked about the three broad sources of inspiration? Well, here's what happened when we combined the three sources—direct, tangential, and abstract—with one item from each of the three parts of the inventory—physical, functional, and emotional.

| Physical | Where are there other places that have **books**? | Direct: other libraries Tangential: bookstores Abstract: yard sales |
| Functional | What are other places that include **searching for information**? | Direct: Internet search engines. Tangential: information kiosks at an airport. Abstract: the detective unit at the police station |

Emotional	Where else do you find **membership, belonging,** or **community**?	Direct: A chain like Blockbuster. Tangential: your $39.99/month local independent gym. Abstract: the National Hockey League Hall of Fame

As a member of Richmond's chamber of commerce, I can tell you that conversations like the ones I'm describing in this section have helped revitalize the city's downtown. Getting city leaders together to create a new future for the city hasn't always been easy. But making it a priority to think about things differently has helped Richmond become one of the best places to live and work in the United States. (Next time you're in town, be sure to stop in at Lulu's on 18th Street and ask for Steve. His meatloaf is to die for. Be sure to tell him Andy sent you.)

Two: I Feel, I Need, I Want

This mechanism is best used during insight gathering and idea development. To use it, you ask participants to explore human motivations by carefully observing what people feel, what they need, and what they want. How do people meet their functional and emotional needs? When do feelings, needs, and wants become actions? This process has three parts:

- *Observe:* Examine the environment and the people around you. Create a list of the behaviors, words, and acts you're seeing.
- *Infer:* Next to each act, behavior, or conversational nugget, write down the unspoken feelings, needs, and wants of the people you observe.

- *Apply:* Apply those observed motivations to your objective. What feeling or desires have you yet to consider about your customer?

Not long ago, we teamed up with a major international pharmaceutical company to explore the company's brand and the types of emotional connections it was making with customers. Standing on the corner of Pico and Robertson in Los Angeles, we asked a number of senior marketers to examine the world around them through emotional lenses. When they saw a woman walk up to a homeless man and give him a dollar, they recorded their thoughts about her behavior, body language, and actions.

We then used those thoughts to explore her underlying emotions. What was she feeling, needing, wanting? Did she give the dollar because she felt empathetic and giving a dollar doesn't take much time? Or was she in a way playing to the bystanders, showing them that she's a good person—maybe a better one than they are? The discussion lasted for an hour, and eventually, dissecting the woman's needs, feelings, and wants as a person uncovered a completely new set of emotional triggers that my clients were able to apply to their brand. The experience allowed them to move beyond just considering functional needs to looking at deeper emotional desires and needs. They eventually landed on a successful communications campaign with this basic message: "You do so much for your family and your community, so do something for yourself; you deserve it."

How can you put this mechanism to work in your organization? Take seven minutes and go through the process outlined above. Go ahead. Write down what you're feeling, needing, wanting. Consider the motivations behind those desires, and then determine how that information can be applied toward achieving your objectives. Imagine competing with other man-ufacturers only on a functional and technical level; only so much differentiation is possible. Once you start to compete on an emotional level, the opportunities to outshine the competition are huge.

Three: Worst Idea

We first discussed the benefits of bad ideas back in Chapter Two, where we talked about the importance of encouraging people to skin their knees in a culture of innovation. For many people, generating ideas can be an uncomfortable expe-rience, especially in group settings, or they hesitate to share their thoughts for fear of being criticized by their team or their clients. Worst Idea is designed to help bypass self-censors and worries about what everyone else will think of you. Any and all filtering is counterproductive, so let the deliberately bad ideas fly, no matter how unrealistic, logistically impossible, or horrible to contemplate.

Worst Idea is a frame of reference; you start, as you might guess, by coming up with the worst ideas you can think of. Then, by identifying any positive opportunities hidden in the bad ideas, you gradually transform them into good (or at least better) ones. Here's the basic outline of the process:

1. *Objective:* Define your objective.
2. *Worst ideas:* Create an inventory of the worst ideas that would address that objective.
3. *Good ideas:* Transform the worst ideas into good ones by identifying the positive aspects.

Business tends to breed ego and fear. So when a team is playing it safe and repeating the same tired old ideas, we've found that this exercise comes as a welcome jolt that can help move the group from where they are toward inspiration.

Remember the hooker doll from the previous chapter? Here's one more example of how the worst idea can often lead to great results. The issue: How do you refresh a product that has a generations-long history and an enormously strong reputation? The answer: you sit on a bench in Central Park and look at more stuff.

In 1999, we were working with the Woolmark Company, the wool manufacturing trade group, to promote a new blend of all-season wool. Woolmark wanted to change the image of wool from the hot, itchy, coarse material that our grandfathers wore in the winter to a versatile, stylish material that could be worn all year long by fashion-conscious consumers. Woolmark wanted major national media attention on a shoestring budget. Oh, and it wanted to do this during Fashion Week in New York City, a time when every rag merchant in the world is competing for the same eyeballs (and dollars).

Our team sat on a bench in Central Park, debating thoughts and ideas (remember, Henning is listening, so no quick solutions) like a roomful of coffee-fueled, bleary-eyed comedy writers trying to put together the opening skit of *Saturday Night Live*. Eventually, someone said, "Let's run a giant herd of sheep through Times Square and disrupt traffic."

We just about died laughing, imagining hapless tourists and irate commuters fleeing from a wooly stampede. It was a terrible idea. But as we joked more about the herd, an idea started to take shape. We agreed that as crazy as it sounded, we needed to get sheep out on the streets of New York City to start a new conversation around wool. A few hours later, enjoying our warm Coke and hotdogs in Central Park, we saw a dog walker walking at least ten dogs. That was it. "Hey," someone said. "What if we put sheep on the end of those leashes?" And right there, Sheepwalk was born.

We hired gorgeous models wearing beautiful, elegant, all-season wool suits and dresses. And we gave each one a sheep on a leash and instructions to walk up and down Madison Avenue as if they were out with their coiffed Bichon Frise. I'm sure you can imagine the reactions from passersby and the number of "What the . . . ?" looks they got. And every time that happened, the models would tell the person about the benefits of all-season wool.

Sheepwalk was nothing short of a huge success. Media coverage extended as far as Australia and included the *Today Show,* the *New York Times*, and the Associated Press newswire. Woolmark got a 30:1 return on its investment and was beyond pleased. The Sheepwalk campaign fundamentally changed the conversation about wool in the fashion industry, and completely reshaped consumers' buying habits.

So the next time you're in a situation where you need to come up with creative ideas, start with the worst ones you can think of. Then think of Sheepwalk.

Four: Deconstruct — Reconstruct

This mechanism is great for reinventing business models and processes. Begin with a list in which you break your objective down into its fundamental parts in three areas: physical, functional, and emotional. Then create a large inventory of ideas by "reconstructing" the components in four ways: exaggerate, eliminate, substitute, and simplify.

1. *Objective:* Define your objective.
2. *Deconstruct:* Create an inventory of all the physical, functional, and emotional elements of the objective.

3. *Reconstruct:* Take the most compelling parts of the inventory and create new ideas by exaggerating, eliminating, substituting, or simplifying them.

This technique is very methodical and will appeal to process-oriented individuals. It's also very useful for dealing with complex topics. But let's start by taking a look at how Deconstruct—Reconstruct might play out with one of the simplest of all business models: the lemonade stand.

1. *Objective:* Reinvent the lemonade stand.
2. *Deconstruct:* Here are some of the components that make up a lemonade stand:

lemons	water	ice
tart flavor	sugar	stand
street corner	sign	lukewarm water
a hand-drawn sign	hot day	summer
pitcher	hours of operation	paper cups
Mom	spontaneity	money
neighbors pretending to be thirsty		

3. *Reconstruct:* Now let's reconstruct the stand, but with a few adjustments.
- **Eliminate**
  Instead of the **street corner**, what if we offered a lemonade delivery service to nearby construction sites?
  Instead of **money,** we could use a barter system and let kids trade other things (used books, recycled cans, candy, and so on) for a refreshing drink.
- **Simplify**

Hours of operation. Right now the stand is open at random times. Let's create regular business hours and post flyers around town so that commuters will know where and when to find us.

Water and ice cubes. Consolidate by making lemonade popsicles.

- **Substitute**

Instead of **lemons,** let's use limes and make limeade.

Instead of **liquid,** let's use gelatin and lime and make slime-ade.

- **Exaggerate**

Tart. Create pucker-packed, super-tart lemonade.

Stand. Create a stand that spans the street like the finish line to a race, or set up a speed bump made out of lemons, to slow traffic, increase awareness, and drive sales.

Okay, that was a simple example; but as I said, Deconstruct—Reconstruct can be used to generate complex ideas.

When Ed Sutt came back from a quick trip to the U.S. Virgin Islands in 1995, he wasn't sporting a tan and a hangover. Instead, he returned with the beginnings of a project that would consume him for eleven years and would ultimately reinvent a twenty-five-hundred-year-old tool that no one else thought could (or needed to) be reinvented: the nail.

Sutt had gone to St. Thomas to survey the damage wrought by Hurricane Marilyn, which had leveled 80 percent of the buildings on that island. What he found was counterintuitive: it wasn't the *wood* in those buildings that was failing under the strain of the wind; it was the *nails*.

Sutt decided to learn and test everything about nails. He started by deconstructing the nail into its most basic components: the metal, the shank, and the head. He then began experimenting and found that nails fail for several reasons. Sometimes the metal is too weak or brittle to withstand the side-to-side movement caused by hurricanes and earthquakes. Other times, the head of the nail pulls right through the wood it's supposed to be securing. And sometimes the pressure on the nail is so strong that the shaft of the nail comes cleanly out of the wood into which it was hammered—just as it would if you used a crowbar. (Using our model, this phase of research would have been part of the physical and functional inventories. The emotional component was already clear: people want to keep their homes and to protect the lives of their loved ones.)

Through more research and trial and error, Sutt and his team found a certain alloy that allowed nails to be flexible enough to withstand side-to-side motion, yet strong enough to bear adequate weight. First problem solved. They experimented with various head-to-shank ratios and found that a bigger head prevented the pull-through problem. Sutt's team made the nail heads as big as possible, given the size restrictions of the nail guns that most contractors use. To keep the whole nail from pulling out, they tried adding barbed rings to the shank, but they found that they couldn't go all the way up the shank, or the hole would be too large to hold the nail. The team's breakthrough came when they realized that adding a little threading (like a screw) to the top of the shank cause the nail to turn slightly and lock into place. The HurriQuake nail was born.

Sutt's nails double the strength of houses during hurricanes and make structures 50 percent more likely to withstand an earthquake intact. In fact, they're so effective that insurance rates for new construction in many disaster-prone areas are affected by whether or not the builder used HurriQuake nails.[2]

Five: Forced Connection

Forced Connection is an idea generation tool that uses abstract juxtapositions as inspiration for new ideas. It's great for when you feel stuck, and you can practice it anywhere, anytime. This is LAMSTAIH in its purest form. For a lot of people, Forced Connection is counterintuitive, but with a little practice it gets easier. History is full of random and purposeful forced connections that spawned remarkable ideas.

Putting Forced Connection into play is pretty simple: pick a random object or an object that is slightly related to your objective and create a physical, functional, and emotional inventory.

Because this is such an important mechanism, I want to give you several examples. Here's the first:

Objective	Customer experience at a bank
Object	Hot cup of coffee
Inventory	Physical: Hot, steaming, contained, brown, liquid. Functional: Wakes one up; is sipped and swallowed; can burn you. Emotional: Soothing; part of a ritual; people take their coffee in a certain way; part of their identity
Ideas	We need to create products and services that are modular and adaptable, so people can fit their banking into their routines and their sense of self. One size does not fit all.

In our Richmond library example, let's use as our object a Sharpie permanent marker sitting on a desk in front of you:

Objective	Drive traffic to library
Object	Sharpie permanent marker
Inventory	Physical: Plastic, black and gray, lightweight. Functional: Is great for writing large letters, good for use with an audience; slowly loses ink; records ideas and observations; shares information. Emotional: Bold statements, power, making your mark permanently
Ideas	Put up whiteboards in the library for sharing favorite books or ideas; include comment cards in the back of each book for members of the community to write their Amazon-style reviews. The characteristic of writing embodied by a marker might lead you to create an idea around original works. Could the public library become the bastion for untested, unpublished writers, giving them an immediate exposure to readers who might start a grassroots following?

Okay, now let's move from the theoretical to the actual. Several years ago, Timberland leaders hired my team to help them accomplish three goals: reinvent the yellow boot and use it as an icon to revitalize the whole company; create a new line of Timberland outerwear; and come up with two or three hypotheses that would allow the company to explore new business lines in the future. We spent a full week of total creative immersion at the Equinox Lodge in Vermont. There were thirty Timberland execs and thirty representatives from the company's suppliers—from shoe designers to the cattlemen who provide shoe leather—so we could look at more stuff from as many angles as possible.

As part of the process, we curated a LAMSTAIH room—a collection of hundreds of items and experiences that we hoped could provide inspiration to help us think of outerwear in a different way. Many of the items in the room were directly relevant to Timberland—outdoor-related objects, including a Ziploc bag full of fishing lures. We wanted the Timberland engineers to look at the lures. But much to our surprise, they were more interested in the bag itself and the mechanics of the closure system. That got them thinking about interesting alternatives to the traditional zippers and buttons used in outdoor apparel. Into the product development process the idea went. That forced connection inspired the features and fixtures of their proposed new line of outdoor clothing.

Six: EUK (Experience, Understanding, Knowledge) Event

This story ends with Olympic champions blowing people away on the hit TV show *Dancing with the Stars*, but it begins with twenty marketing executives looking at more stuff in the cramped Manhattan apartments of six twenty-something trendsetters. In between, my team helped the U.S. Olympic Committee (USOC) use strategic inspiration to recalibrate their strategy for reaching the prized eighteen-to-twenty-five demographic that had grown increasingly indifferent to the Olympic Games. What set this story in motion? An EUK (Experience, Understanding, Knowledge) Event, which my team staged with a cross-functional team from the USOC and several current Olympic athletes in New York City.

We first talked about EUKs back in Chapter One, but let me tell you a bit more about how those events work. Our EUKs usually last two or three days and are a kind of total immersion into looking at more stuff. In the case of the USOC, we put ourselves into the homes and hotspots of young Americans, hoping to find insights that would inform a strategy for reaching them—think of it as urban anthropology mixed with spontaneous focus groups, then add a touch of secret shopper. The EUK with the USOC was just one aspect of our two-year effort to transform the entire organization, which contributed to world-class performance and presence at the grandest of all Olympic games in Beijing. But now, back to the EUK Event.

Like many organizations looking to attract young people, the USOC realized they didn't quite understand the elusive "Millennials." The USOC's marketing team is full of seasoned professionals who approach their work with the passion and dedication of the athletes they help send to the games. (Some of them are former Olympians themselves.) But even after studying all the right trend reports, holding focus groups, and sifting through mounds of data, they were having trouble figuring out how to be more relevant to the critical Millennial demographic. The USOC knew they needed to look at more stuff and think about it harder. They did, and then some.

Here are the experiences that we packed into our first day of curated inspiration:

- **Bamn!** Cheap eats from little doors. We visited this novel East Village eatery inspired by the automats that used to be all over Manhattan. You drop in some money and open a little door to get hot comfort food. Instant gratification, affordable, popular with Millennials, and "open *25* hours a day."

- **Tower Records.** We set out to see how a former vacuum for younger people's wallets is adapting to an age of iPods and digital downloading. (Turns out it wasn't adapting at all—Tower Records has since folded—which turned this into a cautionary tale for the USOC.)
- **Urban Outfitters.** New stuff that looks old. We wanted to examine the workings of a popular national retailer and see how independent vintage boutiques have been blown out on a scale for mass consumption. The visit gave us a look into brands, color choices, logos, and styles.
- **Washington Square Park.** The gathering spot. Even though there were twenty of us, we walked right up to groups of New York University students. We questioned them about how they spend their time, what they worry about, what they care about, what they study, where they shop, and what they think about online social networking.
- **Flight Club.** Velvet rope and velvet sneakers. We were admitted into one of the hippest consignment sneaker shops in New York. It's got a door buzzer, a bouncer, and a line of Millennials round the block. We talked to the owner, who offered his perspective on edginess, exclusivity, and what younger Americans look for in athletic heroes.
- **Kevan Tucker.** A young writer-director shared his perspective on youth culture gained through his research and observations while making the award-winning film *The Unidentified*. He talked about a generation that wants to make a difference in the world, but doesn't know how or why.
- **Apartment invasion.** Easily the highlight of our day. We went to two different apartments, one shared by three young men, the other by three young women. They were all

in their early twenties, and they let us go through absolutely everything in their homes as we bombarded them with questions. With the guys, we sat and watched the Yankees play. We learned that young women think that novelty ice cubes shaped like body parts are always good to have on hand for a spontaneous party. Just some quality time in the homes of our audience and, with it, a completely new perspective on how to communicate with them.

The next day, we regrouped in an open studio filled with flipcharts and whiteboards to translate our experiences into new understanding for the USOC. The key finding from our exploration was that Millennials get excited about the Olympics when they can engage with the young athletes.

So it was no coincidence when Apollo Anton Ohno (in season four) and Kristi Yamaguchi (in season six) were showing off their moves and making ratings rise on *Dancing with the Stars*. This successful and high-impact attention on the Olympic movement came in an innovative form. The genesis was intentional inspiration, which led the group to put star Olympians into familiar yet novel contexts—and subsequently engaged a whole new audience.

An EUK is LAMSTAIH in its purest form, using targeted inspirational experiences to fuel new ideas. An EUK can be three days or three hours, but it is an essential mechanism for innovation that creates impact.

Seven: Thief and Doctor

One of the keys to creative innovation is exploring tangential and seemingly unrelated fields. By examining sources of inspiration that aren't directly related to your objective, you'll discover fresh ideas. The simple idea of Thief and Doctor is to take an idea from an unrelated business and doctor it up to make it work for your company.

As with many of the other mechanisms, you should start by compiling lists of an objective's physical, functional, and emotional attributes. Next, you list the key characteristics that represent success in your objective, and then the criteria for determining that success. Benchmarking against that list of characteristics and criteria should include diverse examples—particularly ones that are as unlike the context of your objective as possible. For example, what can Jiffy Lube learn from Las Vegas casinos about making an experience more exciting? Here's the basic outline of the entire Thief and Doctor process:

1. *Objective:* Define your objective.
2. *Key characteristics:* List the key characteristics and criteria for what success looks like for your objective.
3. *Benchmarks:* Make a short list of relevant and tangential benchmarks that deliver against the characteristics and criteria.
4. *Benchmark tactics:* Pick the most compelling benchmark and list the tactics it employs to deliver against the objective.
5. *Thief and doctor:* Pick which tactics you can "steal" and alter to meet your objective.

In our Richmond library example, we started the Thief and Doctor process by putting together an inventory of characteristics of an upscale bookstore (with the idea that we'd steal from it). For example, it serves coffee and other beverages in its café. We can play thief on multiple levels with this observation.

A natural first impulse is to very literally transplant this activity from that location to Richmond's library. Yes, we could install a café in the library and start serving drinks and snacks to keep people around. But what else can we steal from the concept and the experience of a bookstore café? How about creating areas all over the library (a place that's traditionally supposed to be silent) where people could talk? And if we really stretch our thievery, we could look at a café as a new revenue stream for the library. Instead of relying on tax dollars and overdue book fines, the café could feature not only drinks and snacks but also art by local artists, music, and other items for sale. This is a very simplistic example, but when you start stealing from your abstract observations, things get really exciting.

Here are two excellent real-life examples of Thief and Doctor in action:

If you don't get the connection between Mr. Potato Head and the employee onboarding process, you're in good company. But these two unlikely ideas came together in response to a major U.S. apparel company's desire to find fresh ideas for orienting new employees. We picked Mr. Potato Head before we met with the clients, because he, quite literally, wears many hats and is a multifunctional kind of guy—a good source of inspiration for the kinds of ideas the client was seeking. But we were completely unprepared for the literalness of the first idea that came from the client group: "Mr. Potato Head should greet new employees on their first day of employment." After that, they headed in a more strategic direction, looking at the inherent attributes of modularity and customization. The next idea was to invite new employees to figuratively wear a lot of different hats. That led to the concept of having new hires do job shadowing outside of the department that hired them, and encouraging continuing on-the-job learning. There's not a chance in the world that Mr. Potato Head is discussed anywhere in this company's HR manual. But it just goes to show that a seemingly random item, thoroughly examined and mined for inspiration, can provide fodder for some pretty sound orientation practices.

Back to the case of Trustmark, the century-old insurance company in the Midwest. With around $2 billion in annual revenues and more than four thousand associates across the United States, the organization was comfortable. But growth was flat. The company's own forecasting showed that its industry niche was becoming obsolete.

We hit the streets of Chicago, and on Michigan Avenue we visited an Apple store and a CompUSA that were just a few doors apart. We asked the client's team to spend some time in each store, interact with the products, talk with the staff, and consider the differences. After about an hour, we regrouped and asked for their observations. CompUSA felt like a warehouse full of commodities. The products were crammed together and hard to compare. The staff were uninterested and disorganized. The Apple store was very different. The staff were engaging. We could walk up and try out any item in the store. The word *computer* was nowhere to be seen. Instead, the signs read Music, Video, Connect, and so on.

At this point, our client group was on the edge of an insight they could steal. They just needed a little push. We asked them, "What do those observations mean for your business?" They replied by saying that insurance is a commodity, just like electronics, but that, unlike CompUSA, Apple was selling an experience and a lifestyle—something beyond the product itself. They also could see that they were the CompUSA of the insurance business. (A brief aside to that story: at one point, the CompUSA store manager came up to us and said, "I noticed that you've been coming in here a lot and then going down the street to the Apple store. We're not going to make it, are we?" He was dead right. CompUSA would go on to falter and liquidate more than one hundred stores, including the one on Michigan Avenue. The company and brand were eventually sold, and as of 2010 were in the process of being reinvented.)

This comparison began a process for translating the successful qualities, insights, and approaches within retail electronics to a waning insurance industry. Within eighteen months, Trustmark had created several new products and services that helped the company go beyond the product and create a lifestyle of financial security and performance for the company's customers.

Eight: Stop, Start, Continue

Some people equate innovation with newness, so when planning for action, many individuals and teams spend a disproportionate amount of time focusing on all the new steps they need to take: new research, new sales strategy, new distribution channels. These are the things that they need to "start." It's natural to feel as though embarking on a new task is progress toward a new outcome. But sometimes, a keen focus on the "start" aspects of that progress blocks our view of the things we need to *stop* doing, as well as those that we should *continue* doing. Great innovations can come without any new activities whatsoever. They can build on existing successes and benefit from ceasing some efforts.

Here's a story that illustrates what I mean. Magician and expert mind-manipulator Derren Brown exposes one of the mysteries of human perception. After placing a cash-filled wallet on London's busy Regent Street, Brown draws a chalk circle around it and walks away. From a distance, he watches as pedestrians walk by without picking it up—all day long, most of them ignore it completely. The chalk line around the wallet creates a mental barrier strong enough to thwart the natural human impulse to pick up the wallet.[3]

We tend to draw circles—mental barriers—around ourselves when it comes to exploring new ideas or possibilities. These circles—things like a tight focus on new resources, initiatives, and so on—can prevent you from taking risks, innovating, or fully realizing your creative potential. What artificial barriers are you placing around your creative process? What would you and your organization gain if those barriers were removed? Here's how to use Start, Stop, Continue to find the answer to those questions:

1. *Goal:* Articulate your goal.
2. *Stop:* In order to make your idea or aspirations a reality, what will you need to stop doing? What distraction do you need to avoid? What is outside your core promise of value? What behaviors and language will have to end?
3. *Start:* What new resources (time, treasure, talent) will be needed to achieve your goal? What new partners will need to be involved?
4. *Continue:* What are you doing really well right now that supports your goal? What is at the core of your business? What gives you and your team energy and passion?
5. *Drill down:* Pick the most compelling actions from points 2–4 and create another layer of detailed actions that you map across an initial timeline.

This mechanism is designed to be used as a discussion, behavior, or Blueprinting action step. (You'll learn more about Blueprinting later in this chapter.) Once you've identified several promising ideas that meet the predetermined success criteria, use Stop, Start, Continue to take an initial look at actions required to make the idea reality.

Filter Your Ideas

Okay, all you analytical types who have been driven mad by all the divergent thinking: now is the time for you to shine. In this stage, you cull through the massive inventory of ideas you've come up with to find the ones that will meet your original success criteria and resource restrictions while delivering the greatest innovation.

Which ideas fit within the parameters—budget, timeline, target market, brand, and so on? If all you have is six months to complete your project, there's no sense in developing ideas that will take longer than that. And if you have a budget of only $2 million, you'll be wasting everyone's time pursuing ideas that will cost much more than that. The most direct way to tackle this process is to list your success criteria and parameters, then check your ideas against the list.

Each business objective will come with its own set of filter criteria, but challenge yourself and your team to look beyond the standard return-on-investment lens.

Consider these questions as well:

- Is the solution on-brand or off-brand? Does it really elevate your overall brand?
- Does the idea truly impact your end customer's experience?
- Is it a one-off solution or an integrated, elegant solution?

- Is the idea strategic or tactical? Or both?
- What is the impact that you will be able to measure? And what will you never be able to measure?
- What does your gut say?
- To make it happen, what will you have to build, borrow, or buy?
- Is this idea truly disruptive? Is it incremental, break-through, or transformational?

Although it sounds a little analytical, the filtering stage isn't devoid of passion or creativity. In fact, it's really quite the opposite: you are preparing to champion the ideas you select.

Use Blueprinting to Bring Ideas to Life

Once you've selected the most promising ideas from the various mechanisms you've used, you need to turn your ideas into reality. How? Through a process we call *Blueprinting*. Depending on your specific objectives, a blueprint can take all sorts of forms. But all solid blueprints contain the following core elements:

- **State it**
  This is the simple idea statement we talked about at the opening of this chapter: "In order to _____, we will _____." Every great idea needs a simple articulation that sets up the action you will take and outlines why you are doing it. If you can't complete this sentence, you might not have a solid idea. Remember that this is your chance to make something that currently exists only in your mind feel real and tangible to other people.

- **Paint it**

  Describe the idea in enough detail that an average person could understand its basic components. Think of this as being like an "elevator pitch," when you have only a few moments to explain something to another person. Avoid jargon and business-speak (including the term *elevator pitch*).

- **Preach it**

  The idea you chose made it through a rigorous process, so there must be something exciting about it. Explain a reason (or reasons) for believing in the idea. What's at stake? Sell the benefits of your solution. We often find that ideas live and die based on their spokesperson's ability to persuade. Don't let a good idea fail due to lack of passion.

- **Live it**

  Outline the important details: Who will make this idea come to life? Who will see the benefits? How will internal and external behaviors have to change?

- **Do it**

  A blueprint isn't a full tactical rollout plan, but it needs to include some initial action steps that your team can begin executing. Think of quick wins that build momentum and keep your team engaged as you define all the specific components of a full plan.

- **Name it**

  A good idea needs a concise and memorable name, but don't get caught up and spend too much time on it. Wait until you have completed the rest of the blueprint. Do not start your blueprint process worrying about a catchy title for your idea.

To make this a little more concrete, here's what a blueprint for the Richmond library would look like:

- **State it**
  To drive traffic to the public library, we will start serving drinks and snacks.
- **Paint it**
  We can repurpose an existing area of the library to become a functional coffee and beverage bar. We will create a comfortable seating area where students can study and socialize. Revenues from selling coffee could offset our investment.
- **Preach it**
  Bookstores are popular with students and young professionals. They hang out there for hours. The coffee bar is always full because it is often where the prime seats are. The library can become more inviting and relevant by creating a similar atmosphere. Students organize their schedules around food, so any opportunity to fill that need while meeting another need will be a win for them.
- **Live it**
  We will need to find a beverage vendor and train our staff to serve drinks. We can form a small internal committee to lead the effort. Our behavior will have to change. We might have a noisier environment inside the library and will have to balance that with accommodating those who need quiet.
- **Do it**
  Find out about health code requirements and other necessary permits. Develop a Request for Proposals for beverage vendors and any necessary construction. Start telling library patrons and send the message to schools that the idea is in

the works. Gauge their reactions and ask them for feedback on what the end product should look like.

- **Name it**
  Books and Beans Café.

Okay, Now You Try . . .

Before we move on to the next M, Measurement, take a minute to think about the mechanisms you're using to promote creativity and innovation. Ask yourself these questions:

- How many tools do you have to create ideas? How often do you use them?
- How often do your teams share ideas in person, over the phone, via e-mail?
- Do you have an idea shuttle—people simply stand at the stop, then get picked up and dropped off for an engineered experience? Or do people map their own journeys and experiences?
- Are your buildings named Q543-9A or the Sultan's Sauna?
- How quickly do you go from identifying an opportunity to applying filters to find a solution?

CHAPTER 4

Measurement

Measurement takes into consideration qualitative and quantitative performance and provides individuals and organizations with guidance and critical feedback. The type of measures that you put in place at an organizational level send a strong signal of what is important and where people should focus their passion and energy.

The first recorded game of baseball was played in New York in 1846. But the sport didn't really catch on until an English transplant named Henry Chadwick came along. One of the country's first sportswriters, Chadwick delivered baseball coverage for the New York *Clipper* that helped make the game "America's pastime." Chadwick was also an amateur statistician, and from the beginning, he was fascinated with using numbers to determine which players did the most—or least—to help their team. He's considered the father of the box score, batting average, and earned run average. Far more interested in hits, home runs, and the movement of players on the field, Chadwick left something out of his measurements—the walk. He thought it was so unimportant that it didn't even count as an at-bat.[1]

Chadwick's numbers soon became baseball's de facto rating system. Fans used them to rate players. Team owners began using them to set salaries, and players changed the way they played to rack up the stats. Things stayed that way for about 140 years, until Billy Beane came along. Beane, who became general manager of the Oakland A's in the late 1990s, realized that a walk is as good as a single, and created a new statistic: on-base percentage (OBP), which reflected the total number of times a player didn't make an out—hits, walks, and getting hit by a pitch. Using that new number, Beane came up with a very different way to measure players' offensive performance. He used his OBP and a few other creative numbers to put together pennant-contending teams for a fraction of what many other clubs were spending. It took quite a few years for the fans—and then other GMs—to catch on to Beane's methods. But eventually, they did.[2] (To get a sense of how revolutionary Beane's idea was, read Michael Lewis's book *Moneyball*.)

The old adage "what gets measured gets done" is exactly right. It's true in sports and even truer when it comes to measuring individual achievement in business. And the problem in both areas is that people shape their games and build their careers and bank accounts by adjusting their behavior to fit the criteria they're judged by. Think about the controversies swirling around "teaching to the test" in America's public school systems to consider the implications of this issue.

And what happens to people who don't align their behavior to the prevailing criteria? Well, take pitcher Tommy John. Over a career that lasted twenty-six seasons, John racked up very impressive numbers in several categories that are typically used to rate pitchers, but he's never been voted into the Hall of Fame. John won more games, pitched more complete games and more total innings, and had a lower earned run average than many pitchers who are already in the Hall. He had good control and a mean sinkerball that forced batters to hit the ball on the ground. But John was never a flashy pitcher. He didn't throw ninety-mile-per-hour fastballs and didn't strike out a lot of guys. So even though Tommy John outshone many other Hall of Famers, he never made the cut because he didn't have the "right" stats. Strikeouts and speed get noticed. Consistency and longevity don't.

How many pitchers out there are trying to increase their speed and rack up strikeouts instead of developing a more accurate sinkerball? How many employees and managers are keeping great ideas to themselves because those ideas aren't measured or rated? And how many companies are missing opportunities because they don't make it known that they consider creativity and innovation to be important?

I'm afraid the answer to all of these questions is, "A lot." When we surveyed two hundred top leaders who reported that they are passionate about innovation, only *seven* of them said that they measure and monitor activities related to creativity.[3] Measuring creative activities and outcomes is an essential first step in promoting and rewarding them. Without measurement, any creative culture will wither and die.

Set Measurable Standards to Frame Expectations

Just as baseball players shape their performance according to the rules of the game and how they're measured and rewarded, employees respond to official policy. When push comes to shove, individuals support their actions and the risks they take based on what's explicit, not on what's implied. It's clear that employees respond to the written word. It's their backup, guide, and map for how they expect to be judged. Few people err on the side of living up to corporate values like "excellence" or "fun" if by doing so they run the danger of failing to meet a more explicit expectation. Too often the rules and measures of what it takes to be creative or innovative seem like suggestions or shades of gray, not explicit expectations of job performance.

Consider what happens when there's a difference between what a company says its goals are (putting customers first, for example) and the metrics it's actually using (taking the most calls per hour, aka spending as little time with the customer as possible). Mixed messages like these are exactly why Tony Hsieh, CEO of Zappos, the online footwear powerhouse, has to untrain his new call center associates. Although an unbending dedication to efficiency may be admirable in some circumstances, it runs counter to Zappos' ideal vision of customer service, where a call should take as long as necessary. In untraining and *re*training each associate, Zappos sets the expectation that each employee should focus on the experience, not just the sale. Then, one week into Zappos' intensive four-week training program, the company offers trainees a $2,000 bonus to "quit right now." That offer helps Zappos make sure that it's investing its training in employees who will support the company's mission over the long term.[4]

When you look at what you measure right now, is your organization creating an expectation that everyone should strive for an inspired mindset and creative process? If you're measuring only short-term financial returns, you're stifling innovation.

The tools we use in any given situation often define how we approach it. Remember Maslow's famous maxim: "When the only tool you have is a hammer, every problem begins to resemble a nail." It's easy to measure success by the frequency with which we use our tools. Think about a police officer on the beat. Considering the many tools within the officer's reach, it would be easy to define police behavior through the use of mace, handcuffs, guns, batons, and radios.

Lamar Tooke, head of the Virginia Community Policing Association, helped police officers reframe the expectations of his force. He wanted his officers to understand that the solutions to crime aren't in the many tools on their belts. Tooke wanted his officers to solve problems for the community by using their heads, and to turn to the tools on their belts as a last resort.[5]

The same holds true for corporate citizens. Whether it's because they lack the knowledge or training, or because they're overly reliant on familiar tools, individuals in an organization tend to propose the same type of solution to every problem they encounter. In corporate settings, we condition ourselves to measure success by our use of such tools as Outlook, Power-Point, PDAs, creative briefs, brainstorming sessions, corporate policies, peer pressure, rewards, bonuses, and recognition programs. We have to overcome that conditioning and open up our organizations to more and better ways to measure success.

Reframe Measurements to Redirect Focus

Sometimes equally valid measurements can offer radically different perspectives. The Beatles are, arguably, one of the best (if not *the* best) bands ever. You can measure that in all sorts of traditional ways: number-one songs, album sales, royalties generated, songs covered by other artists, and song that inspired one of Cirque de Soleil's best shows ever (and that's saying a lot), *Love*. By all those measures, the Beatles are at or near the top of the heap. By the same standards, the Velvet Underground isn't nearly as successful. But a friend of mine argues that the Velvet Underground was actually more important in the history of rock and roll because they performed such groundbreaking music, with so much passion and purpose, that the band inspired thousands, if not tens of thousands of musicians to follow their own musical genius and form their own bands. He bet me that the Velvet Underground is listed as an artistic influence in the liner notes and Web sites of more bands than the Beatles. (I look forward to the day that some dedicated soul can settle that bet.)

So which band has had the bigger impact? The Beatles, by selling hundreds of millions of records, or the Velvet Underground, by potentially spawning thousands of other bands? That's a tough call: two different frames of measurement, both valid within the same industry, but each pointing to a uniquely valuable outcome.

The point of this hypothetical contest is that not all frames of measurement *are* equal. Sometimes we need to completely reframe what we're measuring—or where we're making investments. At the height of World War II, the British government asked Abraham Wald, a Hungarian-born mathematician, to help assess the damage to planes returning from battle to determine the best places to install additional armor. Through exhaustive number crunching and diagramming, they had identified the areas on the planes that were most likely to be hit, and were ready to reinforce them. But Wald took a completely different approach, advising them to reinforce the areas that *hadn't* been hit instead. Clearly, the planes they studied had made it back with the damage they sustained, which told Wald that the areas that were commonly damaged weren't critical. The planes that didn't come back were most likely hit in the other areas, and that took them down.[6]

Wald's seemingly counterintuitive approach was, in fact, perfectly logical. Has your organization focused its measurements on the wrong indicators? If so, it might be leaving gaping holes in its performance in the marketplace.

Use Alternate Measures to Gauge Creativity and Innovation

Not long ago, *UrbanDaddy,* the e-mail magazine, did a review of Simyone, a hot new underground lounge in the meatpacking district of New York. However, instead of the usual measures (décor, quality of music, cover charge, and so on), it used a completely different rating system, which included measures like these:

People waiting outside at 2 A.M. on a Tuesday: *31*
Massive bouncers: *2*
Hells Angels immortalized on front wall: *10*
Mirrored bricks used in decor: *234*
People inside: *133*
Ratio of women to men: *3:2*
People inside we wanted to see on the dance floor: *68*
People actually on the dance floor: *52*
Percentage of those people who had no business being on the dance floor: *5.77*
Times we were led to believe that hostess was ready to spend the rest of her life with us if we bought a bottle: *3*
Bottles purchased: *3*

The conversation about measures isn't about "right" or "wrong." It's about looking at measures in a different way. In *UrbanDaddy*'s case, the reviewers used something very different from the usual stars, thumbs up, or dollar signs to give readers a fresh take on a newly emerging urban scene.[7]

Consider simple and powerful measures like, "How many minutes a day do we set aside to generate ideas?" Most companies don't track this simple metric, but organizations such as 3M and Google shout it from the rooftops. They ask employees to set aside a certain amount of time each day to work on projects that tap into their personal passions and research projects. Both companies can point to new products and revenue streams that came from this focused mandate to step back from normal duties and consider new possibilities.

Donna Sturgess, the blue noise innovator you read about back in Chapter One, told me that many of today's organizations are too data saturated, favoring spreadsheets and data analysis over rogue possibilities that may not necessarily test well. "Too often, I see employees work to get all the facts together in order to sell an idea within the organization," she says. "But by the time they're done, it's too old and too late and they've been outdone. Despite having the most sophisticated tools and the most sophisticated measures, customers are still in want."[8]

Donna focuses her energies on changing the way people approach success metrics, empowering people to move beyond hesitation and confidently pursue remarkable ideas. If you find yourself overcomplicating the metrics to test an idea, then you've overlooked other ideas that could mean impact for your customers.

It might not have the most inspirational title, but Mary Benner at the University of Pennsylvania and Michael Tushman at the Harvard Business School did a study called "Process Management and Technological Innovation: A Longitudinal Study of the Photography and Paint Industries." It shows exactly how some metrics can dramatically affect (and stifle) innovation efforts.[9] They looked at organizations that implemented process improvement initiatives designed to increase productivity, and found that over time, these organizations tended to focus on "exploitation" rather than on "exploration." This kind of approach rewards individuals and teams for creating innovation quickly through incremental ideas—typically, by tweaking existing products or processes for short-term gain. Focus on these "innovation" or "process improvement" initiatives eventually limits exploration, which requires a bit more time and risk, but is the very thing that leads to breakthrough and transformational ideas.

Measuring the Connections Between Behavior, Attitudes, Innovation, and Creativity

When I talk with clients or groups about using the right measures, I often hear comments like, "It's easy to measure innovation—all you have to do is look at market outcomes. But there's no way to measure creativity." Well, let me assure you that we can. And we have.

Since 2002, through our work with Kim Jaussi at Binghamton University, we've measured the behaviors and attitudes that are associated with creativity and innovation—and those that aren't. Since then, about three thousand individuals in every possible business sector, from financial actuaries to entertainment conglomerates, have taken the survey, and we have a strong sense of the connections and disconnects between attitudes, behavior, perceptions, and reality. I've mentioned several of them in various places in earlier chapters, and we've included an appendix written by Kim Jaussi that goes into the findings in more detail. But here's a sample of what we found, mapped against the five M's:

- Mood: Followers who report that their leaders inspire them to feel more creative *are* more creative at work. Do you actively inspire your team?
- Mindset: Individuals who see themselves as creative are more creative at work if they consider specific aspects of their nonwork experiences when solving work-related problems. Do you apply your passions and interests to your work?
- Mechanisms: Looking at other organizations for ideas is positively related with being more creative at work. How far outside your own company's walls do you look?
- Measurement: When a company broadens its definition of success measures, a new frame of reference often drives new ideas. How has your company reevaluated what has been known as the absolute measures?
- Momentum: Leaders who see themselves as creative catalysts and consider that role as being important to who they are have followers who are more creative at work. Are you a manager or a creative catalyst? Can you be both?

Okay, Now You Try . . .

By now I think you get the point that, at the very least, you may want to take a closer look at some of the metrics you use to determine success or failure, and how those metrics are affecting inspiration, creativity, and innovation—of individuals, teams, and your company as a whole. To get that process going, I strongly suggest that you spend some time thinking over the following global questions:

- What behaviors or activities do you currently measure that drive innovation?

- What "one-degree" changes can you make to drive twice the volume of innovation out of each of those measures?
- What should you be measuring instead?
- Is there a difference between what you say you want and what you actually measure?

Now let's drill down a little deeper. In the paragraphs that follow, I've listed some questions you may want to ask yourself about the ways you measure Mood, Mindset, and Mechanisms. (These are in addition to the ones that are at the end of each of those chapters.) These questions give you a framework for finding new measurements that can drive innovation and creativity in your organization.

Two things to keep in mind as you read these questions: first, they're just offering some guidelines; to make them fit with your organization, you'll need to tweak the ideas and suggestions these questions raise. Second, because every company and group of individuals is different, there are no right or wrong answers here. (That said, the more "none" or "very little" or very low percentage answers that you give, the more work you have to do.)

Measuring Mood

Consider these questions when measuring Mood in your organization:

- How many people make eye contact when you talk to them?
- How often do people say hello to you as you walk through the office?
- How many people work in places other than their desks or at home?

- Do people hide things from their coworkers (snacks, pens, staplers, and so on)?

- How many people walk into your office or cubicle and help themselves to the candy on your desk? Do you *have* candy on your desk?

- Do people decorate their office space with interesting, personal, even challenging things?

- What actions will get a hand slap in your business environment that wouldn't on a playground (things like interrupting, being loud, interacting with people from another classroom)?

- How many "happy days" do you have in any given year? What makes them happy?

- Do you have a place where people can go to let loose a little? (One company I know has a "fighting room," with gloves on the wall, megaphones available, even a viewing area. You don't have to go that far, but you get the idea.)

Measuring Mindset

Here are some questions that will help you measure Mindset in your company:

- How much time each week do you and your team dedicate to working on projects that are outside of core responsibilities, but that you (and they) are passionate about?

- How many projects fail each quarter? (If the answer is none, then maybe you aren't encouraging risk enough.)

- How long can people chat at the watercooler without being afraid of being seen as "not working"?

- Is "reply all" messaging discouraged?

- In your opinion, what percentage of your team would say that it is inspired to be creative and innovative?

Measuring Mechanisms

We've talked about a number of mechanisms for driving creativity and innovation. Here are some questions to help you gauge how well you and your organization use those mechanisms:

- How many ideas did you create today?
- How many times a year do you change desks?
- What mechanisms are you using to inspire creativity and innovation, and when was the last time you reconsidered their effectiveness?

Measuring Measurements

Consider these questions and ideas when rating your current approach to measuring creativity and innovation at your organization:

- Who can keep a jelly bean in his or her nostril the longest?
- Do you measure gross organizational happiness?
- Do you know who the tallest person in your organization is? Who can do the most sit-ups? Who is the best poet? Who is the best songwriter, instrumentalist, comedian, runner, rider, movie quoter?
- Do you measure how many miles your people travel each year?
- What other measures are inspiring creativity and innovation? Should they be finessed or changed in order to have more impact?

Measuring Momentum

We'll talk about Momentum in the next chapter, but here are some questions that you'll find helpful when measuring your organization's efforts to build and sustain creative momentum:

- How many awards or recognition rituals highlight individuals who drive the culture forward? (For example, "Good job to Catherine for hosting the Thanksgiving lunch rather than staying late and pounding out another PowerPoint.")
- Do you make a yearbook each year to celebrate the people, ideas, and events of that year?
- Do you tell stories about the people inside your team's work? Do you appoint corporate storytellers?
- What is your organization's version of the Olympic torch? How far does it travel? Who carries it? How does it stay lit?
- Is there momentum around your creativity and innovation agenda? If not, what bold action or behavior will create it?

CHAPTER 5

Momentum

Momentum in business is the same as it is in physics: a body at rest stays at rest, and a body in motion stays in motion. Put a little differently, momentum is the self-reinforcing cycle for growing innovation that results from actively championing and celebrating inspiration.

Y ou have to give the potatoes room to breathe." That simple statement changed the way that the folks at a large wireless services company think about leading organizations. It came at the very end of a yearlong leadership development program for high-potential executives, which was designed and led by Alicia Mandel and Courtney Harrison. The statement helped launch one of the program's most potent lessons about momentum—the actions, spaces, and conversations that keep innovation and creativity alive and relevant in any organization.

This technology protection company needed some fresh perspectives for its rising leaders. The company had grown so rapidly that everyone felt strained to a breaking point. Courtney brought our team in to facilitate a few of the sessions and lead some important conversations.[1] So, after a morning of lectures at Stanford, we ushered the entire weary group onto a bus and set off to find some inspiration out in the country. We arrived at Green String Farm in Petaluma, California, where we were greeted by the farm's owner and manager, Bob Cannard. At six feet tall, Bob has the deep tan, gray hair, and weathered nature of a man who has spent more than thirty years working the earth. He's a bold visionary who runs an amazingly productive and sustainable organization, and we wanted to see what the group could learn from him.

The participants were as uncomfortable in their (now) overly formal clothing as they were in spirit, skeptical about whether they could learn anything useful about corporate leadership out in the hot August sun on a farm in Sonoma County. And not a very businesslike operation at that; in spite of the fact that Green String provides food to some of the best restaurants in the San Francisco Bay Area, the place just seemed like a run-down hippie commune, with tie-dye-wearing farmhands loading boxes of vegetables into an old VW bus.

As the farmer explained his operations and underlying philosophy, though, the dynamic of the company's group began to change. People stopped chatting with each other and leaned in to hear better. Standing in front of a plot of potatoes, Bob explained how he looks at his farm as an entire ecosystem, not just a factory for producing vegetables. He constantly seeks a balance between consistent, high-quality output and long-term sustainability. Unlike most commercial farms, he plants a row of vegetables, then a row of weeds. And there they were—a row of vegetables, a row of weeds, vegetables, weeds, over and over, as far as the group could see.[2]

Members of the group were shocked at the inefficiency. Couldn't the farmer double his output by skipping the weeds and planting vegetables in every row? Why waste space and labor by planting something you can't sell? These were very reasonable questions from a group of people thinking like managers.

"That's when he told us, 'You have to give the potatoes room to breathe,'" Mandel remembers. "It sounds so ridiculous, but it was such a great metaphor for leadership—the rows of weeds next to the rows of potatoes. The weeds were actually nutrients for potatoes and gave the potatoes room to flourish."[3]

Bob went on to explain that planting row after row of vegetables would overstress the soil and introduce too much risk. "My job is to grow the best crop with the least amount of input like fertilizers," he told them. "And we don't kill bugs here," he continued. Instead of using pesticides, the farmer grows others plants—all those weeds—that attract the bugs and keep them off the vegetables that will end up on a dinner plate. Rather than trying to overcome nature to produce a desired outcome, the farmer embraces nature and uses it to his advantage.

The technology group started to realize that the pressures from their company's rapid growth had effectively made them an organization that was depleting its creative culture. They also realized that they had been fighting human nature by trying to get too much out of their people. People aren't designed to continually operate at maximum speed; it's not the best route to efficiency, and it's simply unsustainable. This wireless services company needed the occasional nourishing "row of weeds" to give its people room to breathe—less structure and more inspiration, instead of more controls and tighter processes. In fact, the trip itself offered the indirect path, the weed-row, if you will, for the employees to make a necessary discovery about their own growth.

Employees are alive, and they need to be tended. Too much stress on the system can deplete any organization's creative energy. Celebrating important moments gives everyone room to breathe, regroup, and grow. Every other driver of inspiration—Mood, Mindset, Mechanisms, and Measurement—leads us to Momentum. Let's look at some specific ideas for building momentum in your organization.

Momentum for innovation comes through celebrating individuals, teams, and the organization as a whole. Momentum is what keeps a culture of creativity and inspiration going—and that's a lesson I learned from my father many years ago.

As an executive at Chevrolet, my father never failed to celebrate important moments with the thousands of individuals who made up the organization. Every afternoon before he left for the day, his assistant, Claire Walacko, handed my father a small note card that outlined the next day's agenda. (Those cards were the inspiration for the Think Cards I use today to record important lessons.) On the back of the card was a list of people who were celebrating a birthday, an anniversary with the company, or another important event on that day. The next morning, before he did anything else at the office, my father took the time to walk around and congratulate those people—no matter how long it took or how many people he had to cover. He knew that those small celebrations played a big role in inspiring the team and building the organization's creative momentum.

Support Autonomy to Give People Breathing Room

An important part of celebrating people is learning to let go, to give the people on the front lines of the organization the autonomy to do what needs to be done. Ask Mary Ann Kehoe, administrator of the Good Shepherd Nursing Home in Wisconsin, and she'll tell you that the day-to-day challenges of running a nursing home are many (stressful conditions, patients with dementia, and many more). That's why she has her employees participate in the Wellspring program, which provides extra training to nurses' aides—the lowest-ranking staff members who are the primary caregivers for patients. The training not only teaches valuable techniques and approaches for patient care, but also encourages nurses' aides to make positive changes and improvements for their patients without seeking higher approval.

Even though Kehoe supported the Wellspring initiative, she was alarmed when she walked into the building one morning and saw big black circles painted all over the floors. Then one of the supervisors explained that the aides had learned, through Wellspring, that patients with dementia see the black areas as unknown spaces, and avoid crossing them. By painting black circles in front of all the emergency exit doors, the aides had created a much quieter alternative to the clanging alarms that used to notify the staff that a troubled patient was attempting to leave the building.

Patients with dementia also often wander into other patients' rooms and take away personal items. So the nurses' aides—again, without any permission—went to a thrift store, bought an old dresser and a few bags of clothes, and set up the filled dresser in the main hallway. Curious, mischievous, or confused patients were then drawn to the much more accessible bounty in the hall.

By removing the need for employees to get permission before making small improvements, Kehoe was harnessing the collective knowledge of those who knew their customers (patients, in this case) best, and encouraging her frontline workers to be more creative and innovative. As a result, not only did the lives of patients improve at the Good Shepherd Nursing Home, but employee turnover rates went from a scary (but industry average) of 110 percent each year to only 17 percent. There's even a waiting list to get a job at Good Shepherd now. Just goes to show the astonishing benefits you can achieve when you finally give yourself and your team permission to take action.[4]

People aren't machines, yet many organizations treat them as if they were. Work has become an endless to-do list of small tasks. Write up a summary of a meeting for your boss. Build a financial model. Go to a meeting. Order a new laptop. Send in your phone to get repaired. Book a flight for the following day. Rebook that same flight a few hours later because the meeting time changed. Go to another meeting. Check with someone's assistant to reschedule a meeting that you have been rescheduling for three weeks now. Overhaul your HR policy. Create a PowerPoint presentation. Go to yet another meeting. Review a different presentation. On and on and on. Is this why you put your feet on the ground every morning?

The comedian George Carlin often joked that school is essentially child abuse. Doesn't business feel like *adult* abuse sometimes? Our overprocessed, hyperefficient organizations keep us busy to the point that it's entirely normal to feel uninspired. But people are by nature curious and creative; if you don't give them room to grow, you destroy something that's at the core of their identity. As leaders, we need to do something about this lack of creative nourishment, or our businesses will not be able to grow and change in the ways they need to.

Inspiration is as natural to us as breathing. But we've forgotten how to be inspired—and to inspire others—in the context of business. With drive and discipline, we can relearn this essential skill and, in the process, build the momentum of our organization's creative culture.

Embrace (and Enforce) an Inspiration Policy

Open the employee handbook of just about any company today, and you'll find all sorts of policies: sexual harassment, dress code, confidentiality, meal breaks, attendance, punctuality, and almost anything else you can think of. HR people and C-suite execs spend huge amounts of time and energy crafting and revising these policies so that employees have a clear understanding of what's expected of them and can do their job with as little confusion as possible. Why is it, then, that no one has created a standard for creativity or collaboration or inspiration? I think these activities are at least as important to the organization's welfare as a rule governing whether or not you can wear open-toed shoes on casual Friday. Time and time again, I hear from leaders and employees alike that the biggest obstacle to the inspired workplace is a perceived lack of permission to create, ideate, or just try new things. Very few people, it seems, feel that they have the authority to get inspired and exercise their creative chops.

Don't worry. I see the irony of linking the words *policy, inspiration,* and *creativity.* After all, haven't I been hammering on the idea that you should never pass up an opportunity to break the "We've always done it that way" habit? And aren't "policy" and "We've always done it that way" essentially synonymous? Yes, on both counts. However, I know that unless you put it in writing, a lot of employees simply won't believe that management is serious about promoting creativity and inspiration.

Just think about the term *employee engagement,* which is supposed to have something to do with keeping people focused, informed, inspired, and on task. A very senior HR director once asked me how her company could improve employee engagement. My first question was, "What do you want your employees engaged around?" After forty minutes of circular conversation about evaluations and industry standards, the real question finally came out of her mouth and exposed her real priority: "How many questions would you put on an employee engagement assessment, and could you deliver that assessment tomorrow?"

I thought that employee engagement was something that builds and sustains momentum within the organization, or an initiative to rally the troops to work differently or become fulfilled or involved in a deeper way. For that HR director (and believe me, she is far from alone in this), employee engagement is just another task—something managers must assess (using a standardized questionnaire) so that they can check "employee engagement" off their list of goals for the year.

In any company, how do you think employees would respond to an e-mail blast announcing that from now on, management supports innovation, inspiration, and creativity? More likely than not, such an uncreative mandate would arouse either suspicion or apathy. But what if a policy like the one shown here was in the employee handbook? Each new Prophet teammate finds a copy of this inspiration policy nestled among his or her benefits papers and tax forms.

The Inspiration Policy

We believe that a company is only as innovative as the people who are inspired by it. Innovation starts by giving people permission to be inspired and to inspire others. Inspiration comes in many shapes and forms, and there is no single, "right" path to finding or guaranteeing inspiration. To relieve any tentativeness our teammates feel as they find their way, we offer this Inspiration Policy to clarify why inspiration is important to us, and how you will be supported and encouraged to develop it in yourself and your colleagues.

What We Expect. Your desk is the worst place to be inspired. To find inspiration you must explore, which is why our corporate imperative around inspiration is Look at More Stuff. Think About It Harder. We encourage you to leave your desk to pursue new insights. We expect you to share your explorations and your discoveries, record your observations, and develop them into ideas. We expect you to collaborate and encourage others to join you. Finally, we ask you to consider your contributions to our company as a whole. You have the responsibility to meet the functional expectations of your role, but you have the opportunity to contribute to the collective creative culture of our organization.

Look at More Stuff. Creativity is everyone's responsibility. Get inspired by:

- Leaving your desk once a day for the express purpose of feeding your curiosity
- Taking someone with you as often as possible
- Putting yourself in places of great potential
- Trusting your gut
- Changing your perspective
- Suspending your need for a solution
- Skinning your knees (bandages are by the copier)
- Being passionate in your very own, unique way

Think About It Harder. Ideas can go from worthless to priceless in the time it takes to write them down. So:

- Share your very worst ideas.
- Don't judge anyone else's very worst ideas.

- Trust the process. Celebrate the path as well as the outcome.
- Don't predetermine who has a good idea.
- Sell the story and the idea.

Keep the Faith. You are a creative catalyst—don't let anyone convince you otherwise. Therefore:

- When you hear, "We can't afford to do it," respond with "We can't afford *not* to."
- When something starts to feel too intellectual, make it experiential.
- When it gets too functional, get emotional.
- If you don't understand something, chances are someone else doesn't either. Speak up.

As a leader for inspiration, always look for the people who are willing to be bold and speak the truth, like my colleague Kara Franey. At my company, we went beyond a single Inspiration Policy to develop what we call a *people proposition* to drive our thinking for our planning process. A people proposition is a promise or pledge to associates that sets out what the company stands for, what it offers its staff, and what it expects from them in return. Our people proposition is an internal, overarching statement that we use to inform our investment and resource allocation and galvanize the team around the right initiatives and behaviors for our work. Here's how Kara stated it:

Our success is defined by our people. We commit to a creative and collaborative culture where people are accountable to each other and our clients.

To support this vision, we will attract top talent who are passionate, interested, and interesting.

We will retain our team by:

- *Inspiring them to learn and grow, both professionally and personally*

- *Engaging them by welcoming their unique perspectives and providing a variety of client and team opportunities*
- *Celebrating, rewarding, and acknowledging their successes, large and small*

The people proposition doesn't compete with our vision, mission, or values. It's a mechanism to help attract, equip, retain, and support teammates so they can deliver inspired and actionable ideas for our clients. In other words, our people proposition keeps us focused on being the firm we want to be.

Whether you use an Inspiration Policy alone or couple it with a people proposition, you need some type of formal policy that tells your people what types of creative participation you expect from them, and what you will offer in return. A company that can clearly articulate its approach to people is a company that retains and attracts only the best people.

Outline a Path for Passion Progression

Many leaders understand that there's a connection between the organization's growth and the professional growth and development of its associates. But to build creative momentum, you need to consider how your people will progress in the pursuit of their passions *and* their profession. How can you create opportunities for them to follow their passions? This is a question that Rich Rischling, program manager for innovation at GE Crotonville, asks himself every day. Rich helps develop and lead GE's Leadership, Innovation, Growth (LIG) training course. He's one of those rare individuals who understands inspiration's direct connection to individual passion, and he uses that understanding to groom the talent pipeline.

Here's how he explained it during one of our many discussions: "To me, inspiration really is all about the arousal of the mind. It's taking the time to ask an individual, not just 'What interests you?' not just 'What excites you?' but 'What really engages your mind to such a level that you start to pursue it, that you start to leverage that curiosity and tap into your passion?' The inspiration is simply the spark that gets things moving. When you follow it through and see where it leads, that's when you see the impact in your business."[5]

I have always sought out opportunities to engage my passion for creativity and experimentation. When I was growing up in Grosse Pointe, Michigan, I mowed lawns for spending money. I competed with some other neighborhood kids and some professional landscapers, but it was my creativity that helped me win one account—and that account has remained valuable to me over the years in many ways.

One of our neighbors, Peter Schweitzer, the former chairman for North America at J. Walter Thompson, called me on a summer day to ask if I could run over and mow his lawn. His professional crew couldn't make it that week. I jumped at the chance because their house had more than just a front and back yard. It had a side yard as well. I knew that if I could impress the Schweitzers, I could add a steady $30 a week to my well-worn wallet.

I mowed the backyard first and then took care of the front in my standard way, but I knew I had to do something different with the side yard to impress the Schweitzers. Instead of the common back-and-forth mowing that leaves clear straight lines, I started on the outer edge and mowed in a spiral. I kept going until I reached the very center of the yard and then picked up the lawn mower and tiptoed off to the edge so that I didn't leave any mower tracks across my artistic creation.

The Schweitzers loved it, and I won the account. Years later when I started Play, I called up Peter Schweitzer to see if I could pick his brain on the world of business. He was a big shot, and I hoped that he would remember me. He took my call. "The kid who mowed in a spiral, right?"

Schweitzer gave me some great advice. He said that I should always look at my clients in three categories:

- **Revenue** clients are the ones who pay the bills. They're your steady revenue stream.
- **Portfolio** clients tap into your passion and are sexy stories to share with the world, but they usually don't turn much of a profit.
- **Growth** clients push you to develop your skills and increase your value.

Maintaining a healthy balance of all three is the way to run a successful business, he told me. I still think about this framework every morning on my way to work. It's how I decide where I should be spending my time and energy developing our business.[6]

But not long ago, it hit me that this framework can also be applied to sustain momentum and build the passion progression of each person on your team. It can help you find, create, and allocate opportunities for your team that will inspire and encourage them to pursue their passions.

Everyone has a job to do and a set of prescribed responsibilities—call it a job description. These are the *revenue* opportunities, the activities that keep the lights on. They're why each person gets a paycheck and how an organization delivers financial benefits to its shareholders. As a leader building momentum, you need to celebrate how each individual—from the CEO to the sales force to the mail-room workers to the custodial staff—contributes to the overall revenue picture. Part of building a passion progression is empowering people to make these connections. How does the way that the security guard smiles contribute to winning new business? How does the assistant who makes double-sided copies contribute to your profitability? The roles that aren't associated with big dollars add up in any organization.

Each person needs *portfolio* opportunities as well, to give her something—doesn't matter how big—to brag about with her friends, family, and colleagues. Take a new associate to the senior executive retreat. Ask the custodian to sit in on your strategic planning session. You never know what he'll learn there, but giving people portfolio opportunities demonstrates to them and others that your organization believes that everyone needs a dose of pure inspiration, one that has nothing to do with his regular responsibilities or even his professional development. Recognize that benefits of portfolio opportunities aren't necessarily going to be seen as immediately or as quantitatively as revenue and growth opportunities.

And finally, each associate needs the opportunity to work on *growth* opportunities. These are the projects or engagements that enable individuals to develop their skills and harness their talents in ways that aren't necessarily tied to their job descriptions. Growth opportunities might require more training and development, but they engage individuals by challenging them and empowering them to take risks. People going after growth opportunities may fail. But as a leader, you're responsible for making it very clear that failure *is* an option. Without this clear message, individuals will be hesitant to throw their whole selves into the effort.

Recharge with a Radical Sabbatical

Celebrating your teammates in a variety of ways is critical to the group's overall creative momentum, but it's just as important for people (especially leaders) to celebrate themselves. At Prophet, we have a Radical Sabbatical policy, which gives each of us a chance to take a leave of absence to reenergize ourselves and reengage with our passions. I worked for years without stopping to take one of these leaves myself. It felt too risky to physically (and mentally) step away, and I had convinced myself that the entire business would fall apart without me. But my good friends Tina and Michael Brand convinced me otherwise. Both immersed in the art world, they well knew how important it is for creative individuals to be refueled and refreshed. They told me that by never giving myself a break, I wasn't living out the message of LAMSTAIH. Everyone knows that academics can become so consumed in their work that they need time to get away. Why should it be any different for business leaders?

I can hear you mumbling to yourself, "There is no way I could take a sabbatical!" But here's my challenge to you: figure out a way to make it work. If you're that critical to the organization's momentum, then it's essential that you maintain your own level of inspiration and creativity. And you'd better start putting together a plan right now, because it's not going to happen on its own.

Most organizations make accommodations for associates' "life events"—the birth or adoption of a baby, illness, a death in the family, and so on. We need to include a Radical

Sabbatical as a "life event," too. Come on. Will your being gone for a few days, a week, or even a month really take your organization down? Pretty doubtful. I can tell you firsthand that my team has only benefited from my absences, because they learn and grow. In fact, I consider it training toward an MBA—which in this case means Management By Absence. Don't underestimate the power of your team to rise up and take on some of the leadership responsibilities that they wouldn't have if you'd been there. On the other side of the equation, I come back fresh and inspired, my head buzzing with stories to share and new perspectives for continuing to drive growth and change for our organization and our clients.

Over the course of our relationship with BassPro, a few of the executives have told me about the spur-of-the-moment sabbaticals of founder Johnny Morris. Johnny has an application on his phone that tells him when and where the fish are running. Anytime he gets an alert—even if he's in the middle of a meeting—he'll grab his bag and go fishing, knowing that the solid management team he has developed over the years will keep things running smoothly.[7] Yvon Chouinard, founder and owner of Patagonia, writes in his book, *Let My People Go Surfing*, that when the waves are up, he is out of the office. I understand that these examples are a little extreme, but the point is that these moments of refreshment and celebration are essential to feeding the momentum of the business.

If there's no possible way to take a full-fledged Radical Sabbatical, take a thirty-minute "Rad Sab" mini break. Over the past twenty years, I've taken over one hundred drives down Route 5 in Virginia, heading east from Richmond away from the city. The road parallels the James River and takes you past forests and old plantations. I drive fifteen minutes down the river and fifteen minutes back, chilling out to Groove

Armada. It's a great road for thinking and finding new sources of inspiration, and I've had many breakthroughs along the way. What's your thirty-minute Rad Sab going to be?

Empower Creative Catalysts

Our research with Kim Jaussi revealed that only 27.7 percent of all people help others around them be more creative. Are you among the less than a third of people who get their teams energized and motivated to think differently? Or do you leave that to others? Which camp do you want to be in? As a leader, you need to become someone who boosts the creativity of your team. But even the very best leaders can't build momentum alone. They need help from other *creative catalysts*—the passionate people within any organization who embody a creative mindset and know how to inspire others.

Regardless of the formal hierarchy of an organization, you need to identify and empower creative catalysts to shape the mindset of others on your team. Pay close attention to the words you use to describe these people: they're catalysts, not directors or managers. Creativity doesn't thrive well in a world of titles and layers. Many people within an organization may be creative and inspiring, but they probably don't have that specific responsibility within their job descriptions. Identifying these team members as creative catalysts and celebrating their abilities is the way to unleash creativity in others and build the creative momentum of the entire organization.

Keep Pursuing the Bigger Big (Again)

On a late-night flight back home after an exhausting overseas business trip, I had an epiphany. I was exhausted, but I couldn't sleep, so I was pacing the aisles to stretch my legs. I stopped at the small water station between first class and coach, and looked at the passengers in each cabin. I was so glad to be on my way home, and you could see the same sense of anxiousness and hope in the eyes of a lot of my fellow passengers. They just wanted to get where they were going and do what they needed to do, whether that meant returning home, visiting relatives, traveling to a client's office to land a big sale, or preparing to give a speech or nail an interview. As I looked at their faces, I could hear the words my brother, Steve, once said to me: "Everyone is trying to just get by."

I pondered the thought later in that flight, looking at the sleeping face of my seatmate, a weary salesman who had produced from his briefcase a well-worn plastic bag containing pictures of his cats. I realized that there was another side to Steve's comment: people want to do a lot more than just get by. No matter how rich and powerful or poor and struggling you might be, you still want to lead a full life. But the daily grind keeps weighing everyone down. What has driven us all to this point when the only inspiration we have with us is an old plastic bag with pictures of cats? When did we reach the point that we started to settle for uninspired careers that keep pushing us harder and harder with no light at the end of the tunnel? People need much more. They need meaning and purpose. They need energy and connection. They don't only *want* to be inspired. They *need* to be inspired. They need a Bigger Big.

Early one morning in April 1888, Alfred Nobel, the famed inventor of dynamite, opened up the newspaper and read, much to his surprise, that "Dr. Alfred Nobel, who became rich by finding ways to kill more people faster than ever before, died yesterday." The article went on to call him "the merchant of death." In fact, Nobel's brother had died, and the paper had mistakenly identified him in its story. But the words in that premature obituary haunted the famous inventor.

Up until that point, Nobel had considered himself a successful chemist and innovator. Reading his own obituary transformed his worldview, and he realized that he had to use his vast fortune for a greater good, to make the world a better place and celebrate those who make a positive impact on humanity. He established the Nobel Prize. He found his Bigger Big, and the effects of that unexpected dose of inspiration continue to ripple across the world.[8]

Although the inspiration you find might not be as personalized and life-altering as Nobel's, you need to deliberately seek out and translate inspiration into meaning for your life and work. The more successful you are at that effort, the more likely you are to find the new thoughts, ideas, and solutions that will translate into a life-changing impact.

One morning sometime in the 1970s, Dr. Michael Copass, the chief of emergency medicine at Harborview Medical Center in Seattle, was late for work, snarled in traffic on one of Seattle's many bridges. He could see that, far ahead of him, there was some kind of serious traffic accident. He knew that it was going to take a very long time for any emergency vehicles to get to the crash site.

Back then, emergency vehicles were nothing more than station wagons with a gurney and a couple of strong men that would transport people to the nearest hospital. As Dr. Copass sat there in traffic, contemplating the fate of the crash victims, a thought occurred to him. *What if, instead of bringing people to the doctors and the equipment, we could bring emergency treatment directly to injured people where they are? People are dying on the way to the hospital, and we could probably save quite a few.*

When he got to the hospital, he pulled together his immediate medical staff and started bouncing the idea off them. Initially, they were wary of giving any medical responsibility to people who weren't nurses or doctors, but Copass was convinced that they could train skilled people to provide enough care to stabilize patients on the way to the emergency room. But where would they find the right people and the specialized vehicles they'd need? Station wagons just wouldn't cut it anymore if people needed critical treatment.

Copass reached out to other stakeholders in the community, and the fire department jumped at the idea. They were almost always the first on the scene anyway, and they had the right kind of training. They also had sturdy vehicles that could be easily converted for medical use. The police department also signed on and offered up the use of their helicopters to reach especially remote or blocked areas.

This is how the modern system of emergency medical technicians, fully equipped ambulances, and Medic One was born. One man, stuck in traffic, was inspired to make a difference and try something new. His idea may have started in Seattle, but the ripples have extended around the world.[9]

How will you find your Bigger Big? By answering that question, you can build the creative momentum of your own life, and contribute to that of everyone around you.

Create Ideals, Symbols, and Rituals

If we're going to keep our momentum going, we'll need frequent reminders of the habits that drive business success. And when you think about how to celebrate those successes—whether they're individual or team—think in terms of ideals, symbols, and rituals.

Ideals are the things that are most important to you as an organization, the things that define your culture. They can be everything from the way people dress to the company logo to the artwork in the headquarters lobby. At Google, people wear jeans and ride scooters through the brightly colored halls. At most major law firms, you find dark suits, closed doors, and wood paneling. Both organizations are conveying strong messages to their employees and their customers.

At work, my dog, Gekko (whom you met a few chapters ago), inadvertently provided a visual reminder of one of our ideals. My team and I were in a closed-door meeting. There was some laughter and talking outside, and Gekko, who's always looking for a good time, looked up at me as if to say, "Why the hell is this door closed?" then went over and started scratching at the door. Gekko, as usual, was right. After the meeting was over, I circled those scratches with a Sharpie. Ever since then, having a true open-door policy has been part of our culture. And if we ever forget it, we've got Gekko's scratches to remind us. When you think about your organization's ideals, where do they fall along the continuum from Google to law firm? How do you know? And do you have scratches on your door?

If you had to condense your ideals—your entire philosophy, the value you deliver, and the way you work—down into one symbol, what would it be? For our original Play office, it was the red rubber ball, and we never went to a pitch or a meeting without at least one. Almost 100 percent of the time, within minutes of starting a meeting, someone would start bouncing the ball or rolling it back and forth. People had a hard time putting it down. The ball is still a symbol that inspires, a representation of a state of mind in which we're free to push boundaries and make up our own rules.

And that red rubber ball, which began as something to bounce around in meetings, has traveled the world and landed in the hands of everyone from the high-ranking CEO to the curious boy on the streets of Dubai. It's no longer just about the ball.

In a turbulent business environment with lots of mergers and acquisitions, it's sometimes necessary to retire a symbol as part of a move to a new corporate identity. In 1999, the leadership of Nationwide, the insurance company, realized that they needed a complete overhaul of their brand, from their logo to the way they interacted with their customers. "Companies that don't change, don't survive," chairman and CEO Dimon R. McFerson said.[10] But McFerson realized that for many employees, the company's well-established eagle logo was a key part of their corporate and personal identities. Some long-tenured individuals even had the logo as a tattoo or had it painted on the bottom of their swimming pools. A too-abrupt shift to the new "living logo"—the blue window frame—ran the risk of alienating those teammates.

To properly celebrate their new brand strategy while revering the older one, Nationwide pulled off the largest corporate event in its history, bringing together more than thirty-five thousand associates live at headquarters and via thirty separate video conferences. As the highlight of the event, Nationwide execs released two rehabilitated eagles (named Murray and Lincoln after the company's founders) back into the wild. Each one was fitted with a satellite tracking device so that everyone could follow their progress across the country, on the Nationwide intranet. Employees followed the birds for months, a constant reminder that they had to let go of the past and soar into the future.

Consider rituals. Whether we think about it or not, the actions we repeat over and over while we work become rituals. And these rituals are either in service of or in opposition to inspiration and creativity. Do people gather for lunch, or do they eat at their desks? Does the most senior person in the room always start and end each meeting? Your rituals need

---

The Three-Legged Stool

Creating and maintaining momentum is all about the right kind of leadership. I was struggling to help a teammate on a late-night flight back to Richmond years ago. He was having a hard time figuring out how he could make the most impact internally and externally. And, as innovation often happens, desperation and frustration forced me to reframe the issue so that we could collectively have a different kind of conversation. I said, "Think of yourself like a three-legged stool. The legs are passion, expertise, and way. You need all three or you have no solid grounding. And you need to lead with all three."

- So what is your passion? Think back to the Mindset chapter and find your passion in action—the interests and excitement that fuel you outside work. Create a list of words to describe your passion and how it can impact what you do every day.
- What is your expertise? Why do you have the job that you do? Why do you get paid?
- Finally, what is your way? What makes you unique? How do people talk about you after you leave the room? Don't be afraid to ask people. It will launch one of the most profound conversations that you have probably ever had. Further, it will kick-start the momentum and awareness that you need in order to be an inspired leader for innovation.

THINK

to work for you, not get in your way. At our company, for example, one of our rituals is the Monday-morning meeting. But with the amount of travel I do, I miss a lot of them. So when I am in town, I gather everyone together, and we have our Monday-morning meeting on Tuesday or Wednesday or whatever day we can.

Remember Ore-Ida's perfect failure parties where people get to fire off a cannon? Now that's a unique and powerful ritual that transformed the organization. It's also a symbol. And it certainly connects back to the company's ideal of taking risks and pushing ideas forward until they fall apart.

When your company begins to truly activate its ideals, symbols, and rituals, you'll find that they no longer merely exist within the four walls of your company. They begin to take shape, live on, and connect to people, both inside and outside your organization.

CHAPTER 6

Full Circle: The Sixth M

D r. Michael Copass, the founder of Medic One mentioned in Chapter Five, had an inspired insight while waiting in an accident-induced traffic Jam. The insight: rather than bring an injured patient to the emergency care, why not bring the emergency care and technology to the injured patient? He likewise inspired a variety of stakeholders to adopt this new approach, engaging fire departments, police departments, and other hospitals and caregivers. The new approach became the foundation of a larger idea, Medic One. Over time, that new approach grew and spread from one hospital to the next, becoming a movement that revolutionized emergency medicine.

Thirty years after Copass's first inspired insight, Copass himself suffered a heart attack while on his way to work. What came to save his life? Medic One—the very emergency response approach that he helped create.[1] Never underestimate how far you can reach when you become inspired—and inspire others. Ideas that change the world often come back to inspire others and evolve into a movement, the sixth M.

And the movement that you lead is up to you.

Think back to everything you have read in these pages and take action:

Look at more stuff and think about it harder. Say, "No. No. You follow me," and hug a bartender. Create. Lead. Explore. Reconnect. Reveal. Reenergize. Revolve. Ask. Be. Observe. Confess. Defy. Contribute. Discuss. Defend. Commend. Overturn. Argue. Agree. Inspire. Become a curator. Hunt and gather. Get invited back.

Grab a piece of paper and write it out: Inspiration + Creativity = Innovation. I + C = I. ICI. You. Me. Myself. And ICI. We. Us. Unite. Rally. Organize. Deliver. Challenge. Fail. Fail again. Celebrate failing. Find the Bigger Big. Make demands. Own up. Inquire. Require. Resurrect. Reclaim. Relax. Remember Mindset. Mechanisms. Mood. Measurement. Momentum. The five M's.

Answer. Offer. Plead. Play. Connect. Confirm. Transform. Inform. Perform. Wake up. Welcome. Wish. Teach. Triumph. Emote. Evoke. Feel. Excel. Solve. Select. Ask questions to get stories, not answers.

Uncover. Decipher. Focus. React. Respond. Translate. Search for inspiration. By delight. By design. On demand. Go someplace with potential. Get distracted. Distract others. Force connections. Target inspiration.

Get lost. Set out. Adapt. Inflate. Conclude. Erase. Spy. Spend. Congratulate. Correlate. Experience. Compare. Contrast. Convince. Explain. Change your perspective. Be confusion tolerant. Skin your knees. Put passion at your center. Practice. Champion. Catalyze. Experiment like the Alabama hairdresser. Bring your ideas to NASA.

Go find it. Struggle. Laugh. Cry. Disregard. Support. Check out. Sympathize. Scrutinize. Walk, don't run, across the street in India. Take risks. Speak your mind. Go buy a cannon. Shoot it. Shoot it one more time. Now let someone else try. Let someone else fail. Resist the pressure of simply meeting expectations. Suggest Chinese food.

Retrofit. Reply. Attack. Accomplish. Puzzle. Crystallize. Stump. Surprise. Portray. Spectate. Speculate. Ruminate. What's your worst idea? What's the worst that could happen? Send a fax from your dog. Watch it work. Find your passion. Embody your passion. Eat more chocolate. Eat chocolate with bacon in it. One Love, One Chocolate. Oneword.

Babble. Ramble. Suggest. Identify. Indulge. Enhance. Seduce. Steal. Sell. Consider the power of one degree. Explore opportunities. Create inventories. Physical, functional, emotional. Direct, tangential, abstract. Find the space in between. Take it higher or lower. Deconstruct. Reconstruct. Exaggerate. Eliminate. Substitute. Simplify. Nail it.

Look at more stuff again.

Drive. Ride. Sail. Swim. Fly. Perch. Peer. Peep. Dig. Crawl. Walk. Skip. Jog. Run. Sprint. Beam. Go through underwear drawers. Go have a Gimlet in a sleazy bar in LA. Try to find a baby pigeon. Bring a flipchart to a cemetery. And think about it harder some more.

Overreach. Underplay. Do. Dissect. Delay. Mingle. Beg. Ignore. Thief. Doctor. Take. Use. Infuse. Reflect. Attest. Advance. Filter. Forget. Frontload. Decide. Deduce. Bundle. Bond. Don't overthink it. Blueprint it. State it. Paint it. Preach it. Live it. Do it. Name it. Discover the elegant solution.

Think differently. Behave differently. Lead differently. Be like my Uncle Mitch. Shift the mood. Bring the weather. Be the defibrillator. Don't eat lunch in your car. Engineer purposeful disruptions. Ask provocative questions. Make bold statements. Or just walk out the door.

Measure it. Model it. Manipulate it. Manifest it. Mean it. Reframe expectations. Create symbols, rituals, and ideals. Then untrain. Undo. Untie. Unravel. Trade. Test. Debate. Tune in. Tune out. Rejoice. Absorb. Adsorb. Worship creative controversy. Behold the exquisite tension. And cheer on the front line.

Articulate. Appreciate. Postulate. Evangelize. Realize. Build up. Tear down. Throw down. Instigate. Tolerate. Formulate. Nominate. Reward. Recognize. Relate. Seek. Destroy. Testify. Stand up. Lean in. Sit back. Sleep on it. Bow down. Rise up. Step back. See. Capture. Share. Repeat.

My years of experience—both personal and professional—have provided a rich, whimsical array of experiences and conversations, which I harnessed and used as inspiration for this book. My life has been and will continue to be a life of purpose and passion. You can do the same and put inspiration at the center of your life, your family, your business, and your world.

I'd like to thank you for joining me in this exploration of the importance and power of inspiration. Actually, you're now part of what has become something of a movement of inspired and inspiring individuals and organizations around the world. Now it's your responsibility to play the role of curator. As you get out there to inspire others, you'll find that they inspire you right back.

Keep the movement going. Go tell stories. Share experiences. Curate the conversation. Let's meet and have a cold beer at the bar in the middle of all the action.

The Scientific Stuff

My goal from the beginning of this book has been to inspire you with a variety of stories about our approach to innovation. Our framework—Mood, Mindset, Mechanisms, Measurement, and Momentum—isn't something we just made up. It has evolved over years of client work and team collaboration. It has been, in a sense, developed by real-world interactions.

And while it has evolved through real-world applications, we've worked with Dr. Kimberly Jaussi of SUNY Binghamton's Center for Leadership Studies to academically validate what we've been teaching, to deconstruct the 5 M's, and to validate pieces of our framework with academic rigor that withstands peer review.

In the following pages, Kim describes the studies that she has conducted based on our approach and key findings from those studies. The scientific stuff that supports the stories and anecdotes you've read in this book.

Measurement in Action: Building Inspiration Knowledge Through Action Research

Kimberly S. Jaussi, Ph.D., Associate Professor
of Organizational Behavior and Leadership,
School of Management and Center for
Leadership Studies, Binghamton University

Andy Stefanovich and his organization have taken measurement seriously for a long time. So seriously that in fall 2002, they opened their world to me (and the Center for Leadership Studies) as an academic partner in order to measure their experiences and beliefs about the creative process. The statistics you've seen throughout this book are the fruits of that collaboration. We set out to measure the things Play (now Prophet) was training its corporate clients to do and to test things we sensed played a role in creativity, innovation, and inspiration in the workplace. Little did we know how bountiful the relationship, and the data, would be. As of 2010, over three thousand LEAF surveys have been administered in approximately fifty organizations ranging from Fortune 50 firms to smaller start-ups.

By now you've read Andy's advice about having good business crushes. Suffice it to say, I have one on his team, and it's grounded in conducting a large part of my research with them. Our partnership is wonderfully unique because Andy and his teammates continue to sense and articulate the dynamic nuances underlying the creative process in organization, and I then reconcile those nuances with my own thoughts and what has and has not yet been studied by academics across the disciplines of organizational behavior, psychology, engineering, sociology, and education. Science and practice intersect, and together we create new knowledge grounded in organizational realities.

As a result of our collaboration, a number of peer-reviewed national conference papers and publications have been created that offer scholars and practitioners new insights about creativity at work. Some of these manuscripts examine the process of creativity within individuals related to Mindset and Mechanisms. Some have looked more at leading for creativity—how leaders can inspire others to be creative, thereby stimulating the mood and momentum for creativity Andy has masterfully invented in his own organization.

What have we learned and disseminated that's been deemed "worthy" by way of peer scrutiny in the academic community? In the next paragraphs we offer a sprinkling of our findings and the citations for our work, should you be interested in learning more.

We've learned that . . .

o Followership is just as important to consider as leadership when thinking about creating the mood and momentum for creativity, inspiration, and innovation in organizations. Together we conceptualized a model of why an organization needs all followers to play a role in supporting the mood and momentum for creativity. Followers need to be considered not just as effective or ineffective, but even within "effective" as differing in their cognitive style (which we describe as 3D versus 1D) and in their energy level and corresponding style (Red versus Blue). Specific recommendations for each of these combinations are offered for increasing the momentum within each follower as well as for the whole organization.

Jaussi, K. S., Stefanovich, A., & Devlin, P. G. (2008). Effective followership for creativity: A range of colors and dimensions. In R. Riggio, I. Chaleff, & J. Lipman-Blumen (Eds.), *Rethinking followership* (pp. 291–307). San Francisco: Jossey-Bass.

o Some mindsets and mechanisms work together within each individual employee. An important thing to consider is whether you have a creative personal identity—whether your creativity is an important part of who you are. This identity adds more to your creative self-efficacy—another mindset that represents whether or not you believe you can be creative. Further, we found that individuals who see themselves as creative are more creative at work if they apply the mechanism of considering specific aspects of their hobbies and nonwork experiences in efforts to solve their work-related problems. This is the beauty of deconstructing your passion and applying aspects of it to work, as Andy discusses in this book.

Jaussi, K. S., Randel, A. E., & Dionne, S. D. (2007). I am, I think I can, and I do: The role of personal identity, self-efficacy, and cross-application of experiences in creativity at work. *Creativity Research Journal, 19,* 247–258.

o Other mechanisms are also important. And so is an individual's mood. Environmental scanning (looking at other organizations for ideas) is positively related to being more creative at work. And mood matters. We found support for the workplace which suggests that positive emotions matter for enhanced creativity. Andy's words about inspiration and LAMSTAIH fueling creativity are wholeheartedly supported by these findings.

Jaussi, K. S., Gooty, J., & Randel, A. E. (2008, April). *Environmental scouting, positive emotions, and creativity at work*. Paper presented at the Society for Industrial and Organizational Psychologists, San Francisco.

o Mindset alone isn't enough. You have to be able to convince others and sell your ideas. Wanting to learn and absorb more is not enough for increasing creativity at work. Yet when coupled with the ability to express and sell ideas to others effectively, you will observe increased levels of creativity in your work environment.

Jaussi, K. S., & Randel, A. E. (2007, August). *Driven to learn and gifted at selling ideas: Learning orientation, issue selling, and creativity at work*. Paper accepted for presentation at the Academy of Management National Conference.

o Leaders must have a creative catalyst identity in order to create momentum. We found that if leaders see themselves as creative catalysts and see being a creative catalyst as important to who they are, then followers are more creative at work. Also, followers who report their leaders as inspirational in making them feel like a more creative employee are more creative at work.

Jaussi, K. S., Devlin, P., & Randel, A. E. (2006, October 8). Developing those who will lead others towards creativity at work: The role of a leader's creative catalyst personal identity, fun at work, and follower's leader-inspired creative role identity. Paper presented at the Gallup Leadership Institute Summit, Washington, DC.

o "Inspiration by delight" works to create momentum. When employees value having fun at work, they actually do have more fun at work, which helps them succeed in inspiring others to be creative.

The lesson is: have fun at work!

Jaussi, K. S., Carroll, E., & Dionne, S. D. (2004, June). *The real deal rubs off on others: Authentic leadership and the importance of fun.* Paper presented at the Gallup Leadership Institute Summit, Omaha, Nebraska.

o People experience creativity training differently depending on their own levels of creativity. People who are more creative feel that the same training is more effective than do less creative people.

Jaussi, K. S., Dionne, S. D., Harder, J., Carroll, E., Korkmaz, N., & Silverman, S. (2004, April). *Creativity training: More effective for some?* Paper presented at the national meeting of the Society for Industrial and Organizational Psychology, Chicago.

o In a slightly different vein, LEAF-grounded case studies served as jumping-off points for top scholars to consider questions not yet asked about organizational change for innovation.

Jaussi, K. S., Warren, D., & Devlin, P. (2008, August). *Culture change at offices for the future.* Paper reflected on as part of a professional development workshop facilitated by Kimberly Jaussi, Deborah Doherty, Greg Oldham, and Jay Conger. "The Questions We Do and Do Not Ask Regarding Leading Innovative Organizational Change for Innovation" workshop delivered as part of the Network of

Leadership Scholar program and the Academy of
Management National Conference.

Finally, while we included several summary statistics
throughout the text, there are a number of others I found particularly interesting and very much related to Andy's insights.
We have used them to spark discussions in training groups and
classrooms of executives, and I thought I'd share them here
as well.

Mood

Only slightly more than one-quarter (27.7 percent) of the
clients we work with are seen by their colleagues as an inspiration for creativity, as setting the tone for possibilities. That
means just about 75 percent of the leaders, the high-potentials,
the ones the company feels are worthy of the training investment, are not inspiring others to be creative and are not setting
the tone for a possibility-focused environment.

Only approximately 27 percent of those we surveyed report
being inspired to be creative by their supervisors. That leaves
more than two-thirds who are not being encouraged or inspired
to be creative by their bosses.

Fewer than one-fifth of our training participants (18
percent) surveyed report that they are rewarded by their organizations for their creativity. Andy said it earlier: organizations
are not rewarding individuals for creativity.

Maybe people aren't seeing the need for creativity in their
role. More than half (51.7 percent) of those we surveyed did
not see creativity as part of their job.

Almost two-thirds of those surveyed did not see creativity
as part of who they were—of how they saw themselves. Our
identities, or how we see ourselves, drive our behavior.

Mindset

Our data suggest that most of us don't spend time changing our perspectives or considering what is happening outside our own circles. When responding to the statement "I spend time each week keeping appraised of trends in demographic groups different than mine," only 11 percent of respondents in our database reported that they do.

Consider this: our data suggest that our clients are well on their way to changing perspective when they are inside their own company, with their own colleagues; 72 percent of those surveyed reported that they agreed or strongly agreed with the statement "I take aspects of conversations with others and use them as sparks for ideas." But this may be something that just happens or that they just think is happening. In terms of *seeking out* new perspectives, the picture looks different: only 50 percent of respondents in our database could report that they ask questions of individuals inside the company about how they do their job. In terms of the same kind of seeking new perspectives by interacting with others outside the organization, the picture looks similar: just 50 percent reported doing this. About 85 percent of our clients and training participants surveyed said they didn't "seek information on social trends I'm not personally interested in."

Our data support that taking this time for considering ideas isn't something most of us are comfortable doing. Only slightly over one-third (34 percent) of those we surveyed responded affirmatively to "When I have an idea, I like to mull it over." Two-thirds of us are not mulling.

Only 15 percent of the individuals in our database were viewed by others as doing things out of character at work.

Only 7 percent of those we work with are setting aside time to be creative at work. Just 7 percent. If we consider our clients as a fairly good cross-section of corporate America, that means 93 percent of corporate America is not taking time at work to be creative. (Actually, it's probably higher than that, as the people who are reaching out to us are the ones who care about creativity and already have it on their radar.)

Momentum

Only 5 percent of those surveyed are viewed by their colleagues as demonstrating unconventional behavior at work, or the kind of purposeful disruption Andy exemplifies through his stories.

Although our work suggests that having fun at work makes a difference, just 19 percent of those surveyed were viewed as fun by their colleagues.

Research suggests a positive relationship between support at work and creative performance. So how many of us are getting that kind of support at work? Of our clients we surveyed, 53 percent said that they received support from colleagues for their ideas at work; this means, though, that 47 percent couldn't say the same. This means that just about half of our clients are not feeling that their creativity is supported at work—and that's in companies who value creativity because they're reaching out to us to help them produce more of it. Imagine the numbers in companies who aren't reaching out.

In our studies of leaders and high-potential employees, 37 percent were reported as often encouraging others to be comfortable with ambiguity. Those 37 percent are likely well on their way to leading their organization with a mood for creativity and innovation.

What's Next?

As Andy's team and I continue our collaboration and data collection, we find ourselves wondering "What's next?" Our data allow us to stay inspired by that question and to continue to explore it and produce useful new knowledge at the forefront of creativity research.

NOTES

Introduction

1. "NASA to Test Innovative Bioremediation Technique for Oil Spills," Success Stories, NASA Solutions, June 4, 1998, http://techtran.msfc .nasa.gov/new/oilspill.html.

2. Prophet LEAF Survey with Kim Jaussi. Data collected 2007–2009.

3. Paola Antonelli, senior curator in the Department of Architecture and Design at the Museum of Modern Art, personal interview with Andy Stefanovich, summer 2007.

4. "Chef's Surprise," *Time,* February 1, 2004, http://www.time.com/ time/insidebiz/article/0,9171,1101040209-586219-1,00.html.

Chapter One: Mood

1. Margaret Lewis, president of HCA, Capital Division, personal interview with Andy Stefanovich, summer 2007.

2. Kent Liffick, formerly of IndyCar racing, personal interview with Andy Stefanovich, summer 2008.

3. Anita Roddick, founder of the Body Shop, personal interview with Andy Stefanovich, fall 2003.

4. John Unwin, CEO of The Cosmopolitan of Las Vegas, personal interview with Andy Stefanovich, summer 2009.

5. Susan Peters, CLO of General Electric, personal interview with Andy Stefanovich, fall 2009.

6. Duncan Wardle, vice president of global public relations for Walt Disney, personal interview with Andy Stefanovich, fall 2007.

7. Victoria Finn, global creative development director for Disney Destinations, personal interview with Andy Stefanovich, fall 2007.

8. Donna Sturgess, president, Buyology Inc., formerly global head of innovation, GlaxoSmithKline, personal interview with Andy Stefanovich, summer 2009.

9. Thomas Silvestri, publisher of the *Richmond Times-Dispatch,* personal interview with Andy Stefanovich, winter 2008.

Chapter Two: Mindset

1. "Volvo: Your Concept Car (YCC)," *Automotive Intelligence,* March 8, 2004, http://www.autointell.com/european_companies/volvo_cars/ volvo-ycc-concept-04/volvo-ycc-04.htm.

2. Ibid.

3. Ivy Ross, executive VP of marketing for the Gap, Inc., personal interview with Andy Stefanovich, fall 2001.

4. Red Dot, "The Best Designers of the Red Dot Award: Product Design 2006: Daniel Brown," June 21, 2006, http://en.red-dot.org/1839.html.

5. David McDonough, CEO of Trustmark, personal interview with Andy Stefanovich, fall 2007.

6. Robert D. Behn, "Creating an Innovative Organization: Ten Hints for Involving Frontline Workers," GovLeaders.org, http://govleaders.org/ behn_innovation.htm. This article was originally published in the Fall 1995 issue of *State and Local Government Review, 27*(3).

7. For Gallup Poll data, see www.gallup.com.

8. Stew Friedman, author of *Total Leadership,* and Practice Professor of Management at the Wharton School of Business, personal interview with Andy Stefanovich, winter 2000.

9. To learn more about Katrina Markoff and the story of Vosges Haut-Chocolate, see http://www.vosgeschocolate.com/who_we_are.

10. Gilles Barathier's story appears in "Mars in Action," http://rd.mars .com/Canada/en/Mars+in+action.htm.

11. David Storkholm, cofounder, Creative Leadership for KaosPilot International, personal interview with Andy Stefanovich, winter 1999.

12. Henning Sejer Jakobsen, idea developer for the Danish Technological Institute, personal interview with Andy Stefanovich, winter 1998.

13. Kishore Biyani's story appears in Surajeet Das Gupta, "Meet India's King of Retail," rediff.com, January 15, 2005, http://www.rediff .com/money/2005/jan/15spec2.htm.

14. Noah Scalin, founder and creator of Another Limited Rebellion and Skull-A-Day, personal interview with Andy Stefanovich, fall 2009. View his skulls at http://skulladay.blogspot.com/.

Chapter Three: Mechanisms

1. Melinda Brodbeck and Erin Evans, "Dove Campaign for Real Beauty Case Study," *Public Relations Problems and Cases,* March 5, 2007, http://psucomm473.blogspot.com/2007/03/dove-campaign-for-real-beauty-case.html.

2. The story of Ed Sutt's HurriQuake nails appears in Tom Clynes, "Dr. Nail vs. the Monster," *PopSci Innovator,* http://www.popsci.com/popsci/ flat/bown/2006/innovator_5.html.

3. Watch Derren Brown's experiment, available at http://www.metacafe .com/watch/2421839/derren_brown_wallet/.

Chapter Four: Measurement

1. For a biography of Henry Chadwick, see http://www.henrychadwick .com/.

2. Billy Beane's story appears in Keith H. Hammonds, "How to Play Beane Ball," *Fast Company,* April 30, 2003, http://www.fastcompany.com/ magazine/70/beane.html.

3. Survey of FORTUNE Innovation Conference attendees, Spring 2008.

4. For more information about Tony Hsieh and Zappos, see Keith McFarland, "Why Zappos Offers New Hires $2,000 to Quit," *Bloomberg Businessweek,* September 16, 2008, http://www.businessweek .com/smallbiz/content/sep2008/sb20080916_288698.htm.

5. Lamar Tooke, head of the Virginia Community Policing Association, personal interview with Andy Stefanovich, fall 2000.

6. I read about Abraham Wald's solution on the Back of the Napkin blog, March 17, 2006, http://digitalroam.typepad.com/digital_roam/2006/ 03/the_hole_story_.html.

7. "Simyone Lounge, by the Numbers," *UrbanDaddy,* September 25, 2009, http://www.urbandaddy.com/nyc/nightlife/7354/Simyone_Lounge_Simyone_Lounge_by_the_Numbers_New_York_City_NYC_Chelsea_Lounge.

8. Donna Sturgess, president, Buyology Inc., formerly global head of innovation, GlaxoSmithKline, personal interview with Andy Stefanovich, summer 2009.

9. Mary Benner and Michael Tushman, "Process Management and Technological Innovation: A Longitudinal Study of the Photography and Paint Industries," *Administrative Science Quarterly,* December 2002, *47*(4), 676–706.

Chapter Five: Momentum

1. Courtney Harrison, the Center for Creative Leadership, personal interview with Andy Stefanovich, summer 2005.

2. Bob Cannard, founder of Green String, personal interview with Andy Stefanovich, summer 2005.

3. Alicia Mandel, U.S. Olympic Committee, personal interview with Andy Stefanovich, summer 2005.

4. The story of Mary Ann Kehoe and the Wellspring program appears in Joseph Shapiro, "Nursing Home Finds Aides Key to Good Care," *npr,* September 18, 2002, http://www.npr.org/programs/morning/features/2002/sept/nursinghomes/index.html.

5. Rich Rischling, global learning and development leader at GE, personal interview with Andy Stefanovich, summer 2009.

6. Peter Schweitzer, former chairman for J. Walter Thompson, personal interview with Andy Stefanovich, summer 1984.

7. Johnny Morris's story appears in Jayne O'Donnell, "Bass Pro CEO Morris Brings Passion for Fishing to Job," *USA Today,* September 29, 2009, http://www.usatoday.com/money/industries/retail/2009-09-29-bass-pro-ceo-johnny-morris-N.htm.

8. For a biography of Alfred Nobel, see http://www.biographyshelf.com/alfred_nobel_biography.html.

9. For information about Dr. Copass's contributions and the history of Medic One, see http://www.mediconefoundation.org/medic-one/history.htm.

10. "Nationwide Launches New Brand Identity with 'Living Logo' to Strengthen Consumer Relationships," press release, August 30, 1999, http://www2.prnewswire.com/cgi-bin/stories.pl?ACCT=104 &STORY=/www/story/08-30-1999/0001012132&EDATE=.

Chapter Six: Full Circle: The Sixth M

1. This aspect of Dr. Copass's story is covered in Gordy Holt, "Medic 1 Rescues Its Own," *Seattle Post-Intelligencer,* October 30, 2001, http://www.highbeam.com/doc/1G1-79822951.html.

ACKNOWLEDGMENTS

A kajillion thanks.

I believe in business crushes, those people who are a part of your professional life who give you the same feeling as your seventh-grade crush in middle school. The people I mention here have made me a part of their magic, and I am forever grateful: my teammates at Prophet, Bill and Chickie La Macchia, David Storkholm, Armin Brott, Rodolfo Ramirez, Ivy Ross, Paul Westbrook, Stew Friedman, Susan Peters, Andy Berndt, Randy Webb, Kent Liffick, Beth Comstock, Stan Lippleman, Bert McDowell, Michael Brand, Seth Farbman, Courtney Harrison, Alex Gonzales, Frank Mars, Anita Roddick, Duncan Wardle, Steve Stefanovich, Bob Mooney, Dean Panos, Paola Antonelli, Polly LaBarre, John Sherman, Jim Ukrop, The Greenberg Duo, and so many, many more.

A book is a wild beast to be tamed, then unleashed, and my team did it masterfully. Levine Greenberg Literary Agency deserves its word-on-the-street reputation as one of the best in the business, largely based on Jim's freakishly magical ways. Karen Murphy led our partnership with Jossey-Bass with spirit and challenge, and ultimately took us to places we couldn't see ourselves before. Equally important, she made a great team available to "look at more." Special thanks to Gayle Mak and Mary Garrett for seeing us through.

It really is about inspiration, and I'm often asked, as one who is obsessed with the idea and importance of inspiration, who inspires me? Again, a kajillion thanks to those above.

For those who pushed the ideas out of my head and made them something tangible . . . a continuous high-five and hug.

That list most notably includes Ben Armbruster, Robert Throckmorton, Catherine Strotmeyer, Courtney Ferrell, and Geof Hammond. Ben, your months of tireless wordsmithing and making meaning out of thousands of Think Cards is a feat like no other. I spoke and you wrote and the reader thanks you. Robert, Courtney, Catherine, and Geof deserve real thanks for—over the course of a dozen years—creating story and meaning out of our journey at Play, and now, Prophet.

◇◇

Sisters and brothers are super special if you really think about it. They are the people you're set up to share life with, and I wouldn't have wanted to do it without Christine and Steve. My guardian angels, you both march next to me and provide the laughs. And Christine, my partner at Play, without you, none of this would have happened . . . smooch.

Everyone should be so lucky to have a companion and partner like my wife, Jill, who's her own fascinating person, while always keeping my passions and pursuits at heart. I don't gamble, because I hit the jackpot with her. Coolest-woman-in-the-world award goes to you. And together we hit the jackpot in our two daughters, who are now the inspiration to continue on this important life journey. Big questions inspire, and they continue to write that book for all of us.

I was once asked, after a speech, "Where do you come from?" Physically and spiritually, my mother, Barbara, and my father, Steve. No other words can describe my love and appreciation for what I call daily the best parents in the world. My passion, hopes, and beliefs fall right from their tree, and I wouldn't want it any other way. The challenge is enormous—working every day for my daughters to feel the same way. (Because of Jill, we have a pretty good chance.)

ABOUT THE AUTHOR

Andy Stefanovich, chief curator and provocateur at Prophet, has earned a reputation as one of the most disruptive and effective advisers in business. He has spent the past twenty years helping companies like GE, Nike, Procter & Gamble, the United States Olympic Committee, and the Coca-Cola Company drive innovation from the inside out—enriching their people and driving marketplace growth. Andy's true passion lies in guiding clients through the powerful evolution from inspiration to innovation. He teaches practical skills, leadership behaviors, and specific processes for developing and implementing ideas at work.

Andy has been featured on CNBC as a nationally recognized innovation thought leader, and acts as visiting professor for many leading universities, including Dartmouth, University of Richmond, University of Michigan, Duke, and the Wharton School of Leadership.

In 1990, Andy cofounded Play, a creativity and innovation company that changed the way business does business. While there, he helped many leading companies find ways to inspire and equip their people to create sustainable innovation. Prophet and Play joined forces in December 2008.

Andy resides in Richmond, Virginia, with his wife and two daughters.

INDEX

A

Abstract inspiration sources: description
of, 52; examples to compare direct,
tangential, and, 54–55
All in the Family (TV series), 22
A.M. Cheers, 23
Antonelli, Paola, 13–14
Apartment invasion research, 117–118
Apple, 52
Apple store, 121–122
Armbruster, Ben, 37–38, 77
Ask provocative questions: a list of
favorite, 27–28; shifting mood
through, 21, 26–28
Autonomy support, 147–149

B

Back to the Future (film), 84
Bamn!, 116
Barathier, Gilles, 75
Barletta, Marti, 51
Baseball ratings, 129–131
BassPro, 158
Beane, Billy, 130
The Beatles, 133–134
Beijing, 116
Benner, Mary, 136–137
Big Bazaar grocery stores (India),
85–87
Bigger Big: creating momentum
through pursuit of, 159–162;
description of the, 12; making space
for the, 99–100
Binghamton University, 7, 137

Bionic Wrench, 52–53
Biyani, Kishore, 85–87
"Blue noise," 42
Blueprinting: bringing your idea to life
using, 125; core elements of,
125–128
Body Shop, 31–32
Bold statements. *See* Making bold
statements
Borat (film), 30
Breakthrough innovations, 93
Brown, Derren, 122–123
"Business crushes,"74–76

C

Caesar's Palace (Las Vegas), 32, 33
Cannard, Bob, 144
Carlin, George, 148
Chadwick, Henry, 129–130
Challenging assumptions: avoiding cost
of unchallenged assumptions,
85–87; establishing confusion
tolerance mindset by, 47, 77–88;
"Go find it" game, 79; practicing
confusion tolerance for, 80–84; set
aside time to find options, 77–80;
stop looking for solutions, 84–85;
understanding there are no
absolutes, 83
Changing your perspective: direct,
tangential, and abstract sources for,
51–55; engaging loyal opposition
for, 58; exploring close to home
sources of inspiration, 53, 56; learn

from random people for, 56–57;
producing inspired mindset by, 47,
48–59; thinking about your
perspective for, 58–59; Volvo Your
Concept Car (YCC) example of,
48–51

Chevrolet, 146

Chouinard, Yvon, 158

Cirque de Soleil, 134

CMO (chief mood officer), 42–45

CompUSA, 121–122

Confusion tolerance mindset: avoiding
cost of unchallenged assumptions,
85–87; establishing your, 89;
practicing, 80–84; questions to ask
about your, 88; set aside time to
find options, 77–80; stop looking
for solutions, 84–85;
understanding there are no
absolutes, 83. *See also* Mindset

Conservateurs, 13

Copass, Michael, 161–162, 167

The Cosmopolitan (Las Vegas), 32, 33

Crate & Barrel, 11

Creative catalysts empowerment, 159

Creative context approaches: elegant
solutions, 98, 99; framing
challenges, 98, 100; make space for
the Bigger Big, 98, 99–100

Creativity: alternative measures to
gauge, 135–137; challenge
assumptions and embrace
ambiguity for, 47, 77–88; how
unchallenged assumptions misdirect
your, 85–87; lawn mowing and
competitive edge of, 154–155;
measuring connections between
behavior, attitudes, innovation, and,
137–138; Noah Scalin's four tenets
of, 88–89. *See also* Innovation;
Inspiration

Curators: becoming curator of
inspiration, 11–14;

hunter-gatherer, 14; traditional
definition of, 13; zeitgeist, 13

D

Dancing with the Stars (TV show), 115,
118

Danish Technical Institute, 84

Deconstruct—Reconstruct, 109–113

deRoo, Hillary, 36

Direct inspiration sources: description
of, 51; examples to compare
tangential, abstract, and, 54–55

Discipline of rehearsal, 69

Disney, 37–38

Dove Campaign for Real Beauty
campaign, 96, 98

Dublin college solution story, 96–98

E

Elegant solutions, 98, 99

Embracing ambiguity: avoiding high
cost of unchallenged assumptions,
85–87; establishing confusion
tolerance mindset by, 47, 77–88;
"Go find it" game, 79; practicing
confusion tolerance for, 80–84; set
aside time to find options, 77–80;
stop looking for solutions, 84–85;
understanding there are no
absolutes, 83

Emotional characteristics: description
of, 101; direct, tangential, and
abstract inspirations, 104;
Richmond downtown, 102, 105;
Richmond public library, 103

Employees: empowering creative
catalysts, 159; engaging, 150;
engaging loyal opposition, 58;
onboarding process for, 120–121.
See also Organizations

EUK Event (Experience,
Understanding, Knowledge): Nike
executive team story on, 23–25;

USOC (U.S. Olympic Committee) use of, 115–118

Exxon *Valdez* oil spill: hair solution expanded beyond the, 5–6; McCrory's inspiration following the, 4–5

F

Failures: Ore-Ida's perfect failure parties, 61–62, 166; taking risk for, 59–63, 65

Ferrell, Courtney, 11

Finn, Victoria, 38

Five M's: full circle of the sixth M, 167–170; measurement, 16, 129–142; mechanisms, 15, 16, 91–128; mindset, 15–16, 47–90; momentum, 16–17, 142, 143–166; mood, 15, 19–45

Flight Club, 117

Food Bazaar grocery stores (India), 85–87

Forced Connection, 113–115

Four P's (product, pricing, placement, promotion), 96

Framing challenges, 100

Franey, Kara, 152–153

Friedman, Stew, 71

Full circle: sixth M, 167–170

Functional characteristics: description of, 101; direct, tangential, and abstract inspirations, 104; Richmond downtown, 102, 105; Richmond public library, 103

G

Gates, Bill, 100

GE (General Electric): "imagination at work" mantra of, 53, 56; Leadership, Innovation, Growth (LIG) training at, 153–154; making physical changes to set mood at, 36–37

Gekko (dog): open-door policy inspired by, 163; past-due request fax story on, 64–65

Gerbera daisy bouquet recognition, 24–25

GlaxoSmithKline, 42

"Go find it" game, 79

Good Shepherd Nursing Home (Wisconsin), 147–148

Good-news articles, 42–43

Google, 100, 136

Green String Farm (California), 144–145

Growth clients, 155, 156–157

GSD&M, 43

Gulf of Mexico oil spill (2010), 5

H

Hair mat solution, 5–6

Hammond, Geof, 95

Harborview Medical Center (Seattle), 161

Harrison, Courtney, 143–144

Harvard Business School, 137

Hollywood cemetery (Virginia), 38

Hooker doll idea, 60–61, 108

Hospital Corporation of America (HCA), 30

Hsieh, Tony, 132

Human library (Sweden), 57

Humor: Gekko fax story as example of, 64–65; risk-taking by including, 65–67

Hunter-gatherer curators, 14

Hurricane Marilyn, 111

HurriQuake nail, 112–113

I

Idea generation: eight mechanisms for effective, 101–124; how a one-degree difference can make for, 95; parameters for, 97; risk-taking for, 47, 59–67; Woolmark sheepwalk campaign, 108–109

Ideals: definition of, 163; momentum through rituals, symbols, and, 162–166

Ideas: Blueprinting to bring to life your, 125–128; description of, 92; filtering your, 124–125; four steps for transforming innovation into, 92; mental barriers to exploring new, 123. *See also* LAMSTAIH (Look at More Stuff, Think About It Harder)

Incremental innovations, 93

IndyCar, 30, 31

Innovation: as almost meaningless due to overuse, 7; alternative measures to gauge, 135–137; breakthrough, 93; incremental, 93; inspiration as best way to unleashing, 1–2; of oil spill solution, 4–6; transformational, 94; transforming into ideas, 92, 98–142. *See also* Creativity

Input: focusing on, 6–7; as source for inspiration, 7–9

Inspiration: becoming the curator of, 11–14; the Bigger Big impact of, 12; bold statement on business reliance on, 30; don't underestimate the impact of, 167–168; learning to look for new sources of, 7–9; oil spill solution, 4–6; unleashing innovation through, 1–2. *See also* Creativity

Inspiration Policy: creating momentum through a, 149–150, 152–153; sample of, 151–152

Inspiration sources: direct, tangential, and abstract, 51–55; exploring close to home, 53, 56; inspiration by delight, 9; inspiration by design, 9–10; inspiration on demand, 10

iPod Nano, 52

J

J. Walter Thompson, 154

Jakobsen, Henning Sejer, 84–85

Jaussi, Kim, 7, 137–138, 159

John, Tommy, 130–131

K

Kannon (driver), 77–79

KaosPilot International, 83, 84

Kehoe, Mary Ann, 147, 148

L

LAMSTAIH (Look at More Stuff, Think About It Harder): definition of, 2; EUK Event (Experience, Understanding, Knowledge) as form of, 23–25, 115–118; focus on input instead of output, 6–9; Forced Connection form of, 113–115; how one-degree difference can impact, 95; introducing the five M's of, 14–17; Radical Sabbatical as living message of, 157–159. *See also* Ideas

Le Cordon Bleu (Parais), 72

Leadership: Management By Absence (MBA), 158; remind yourself that you don't have all the answers, 85; rows of weeds next to potatoes metaphor for, 145; setting the mood role of, 42–45. *See also* Organizations

Learning from random people, 56–57

Lemonade stand, 110–111

Leon, Chip, 23

Let My People Go Surfing (Chouinard), 158

Lewis, Margaret, 30

Lewis, Michael, 130

Liffick, Kent, 30–31

"Living library" (Sweden), 57

LoggerHead Tools, 52

Logos, 164–165

Love (Cirque de Soleil), 134

Loyal opposition, 58

M

McCrory, Phillip, 3–6, 8
McDonough, Dave, 56–57
McFerson, Dimon R., 164
Making bold statements: challenging the paradigm by, 29–31; shifting mood through, 21, 28–31
Making physical changes: Building1/Building 2 story on, 34–35; building innovation areas, 40–42; changing physical identity to change thinking, 38–39; Disney's approach to, 37–38; GE (General Electric) understanding of, 36–37; shifting mood through, 34–42; two things to keep in mind for, 34; unique places to have a drink list, 41. *See also* Physical characteristics
Management By Absence (MBA), 158
Mandel, Alicia, 143, 145
Markoff, Katrina, 72–73
Maslow, Abraham, 133
Measurement: baseball ratings, 129–131; of behavior, attitudes, innovation, and creativity connections, 137–138; description of, 16, 129; framing expectations using set standards of, 131–137; global questions to ask about, 138–139; measuring, 141; mechanisms, 141; mindset, 140–141; momentum, 142; mood, 139–140
Mechanism techniques: Deconstruct—Reconstruct, 109–113; EUK Event (Experience, Understanding, Knowledge), 23–25, 115–118; Forced Connection, 113–115; lists and more lists, 101–105; observe, infer, and apply your feelings, 105–107; Stop, Start, Continue, 122–124; Thief and Doctor, 118–122; Worst Idea, 60–61, 107–109

Mechanisms: Blueprinting to bring ideas to life, 125–128; building your context to create, 98–100; description of, 15, 16, 91; don't overlook the space in between for solutions, 96–98; filtering your ideas, 124–125; framing challenges, 100; for generating more effective ideas, 101–124; using ideas and innovations of every size, 93–94; measuring, 141; one-degree difference making an idea, 95; putting ideas in their place, 92–94; questions to ask about your use of, 128
Medic One, 162, 167
Mental barriers, 123
Millennials consumer research, 115–118
Mindset: ask yourself these questions about, 89–90; challenge assumptions and embrace ambiguity for creative, 47, 77–88; change your perspective to open your, 47, 48–59, 88; description of, 15–16, 47; finding your passion to produce an inspired, 47, 67–76, 89; four "thinking disciplines" producing an inspired, 47–48; measuring, 140–141; Noah Scalin's skull project as example of inspired, 88–89; taking risks (skin your knees) to open your, 47, 59–67, 89. *See also* Confusion tolerance mindset
Mirsky, Lauren, 36
Mitch, Uncle, 22
Momentum: create ideals, symbols, and rituals for, 162–166; description of, 16–17, 143, 146; embrace and

enforce an Inspiration Policy for, 149–153; empowering creative catalysts for, 159; using the Green String Farm to teach about, 143–146; keep pursuing the Bigger Big for, 159–162; measuring, 142; outline a path for passion progression to create, 153–157; recharge with Radical Sabbatical, 157–159; support autonomy to give people breathing room for, 147–149

Moneyball (Lewis), 130

Mood: ask yourself these questions about, 45; becoming the CMO (chief mood officer), 42–45; description of, 15, 19–20; importance of, 20–21; leadership role in setting the, 42–45; list of places to have a drink creating, 41; measuring, 139–140; techniques for shifting the, 21–42

Mood shifting: ask provocative questions for, 21, 26–28; create purposeful disruptions for, 21–26; make bold statements for, 21, 28–31; make physical changes for, 21, 34–42; use simple language for, 21, 31–34

Morris, Johnny, 158

Mowing lawn business, 154–155

Mr. Potato Head game, 120–121

Museum of Contemporary Art (Chicago), 11

Museum mentality, 11, 12

Museum of Modern Art (New York City), 13

N

Nail Deconstruct—Reconstruct story, 111–113

NASA's Marshall Space Flight Center, 5

NASA's Technology Transfer Center, 6

Nationwide's rehabilitated eagles story, 164–165

Neon Museum (Las Vegas), 32–33

New York *Clipper,* 129

New York Times, 109

Nike executive team, 23–25

Nobel, Alfred, 160–161

Nobel Prize, 161

O

Oakland A's, 130

Ohno, Apollo Anton, 118

Oil spill solution, 4–6

Olympics, 115–118

On-base percentage (OBP), 130

Oneword, 73–74

Ore-Ida, 61, 166

Organizations: empowering creative catalysts in, 159; Inspiration Policy of, 149–153; Radical Sabbatical policy of, 157–159. *See also* Employees; Leadership

P

Passion: creating momentum through progression of, 153–157; deconstructing, 69–71; developing "business crushes" related to others,' 74–76; innovative pet food manufacture efficiency and, 75; inspiration by finding your, 47, 67–76; integrating into every area of your life, 71–73; Oneword to connect your, 73–74; personal and professional, 76; questions to ask about your, 76; the three-legged stool with one leg of, 165

Patagonia, 158

People proposition, 152–153

Perfect failures, 61–62, 166

Pet food manufacture, 75

Peters, Susan, 36

Philippine oil spill (2006), 5

Physical characteristics: description of, 101; direct, tangential, and abstract inspirations, 104; Richmond downtown, 102, 105; Richmond public library, 103. *See also* Making physical changes

Play: categories of clients used at, 155–157; Gekko fax story on late payment to, 64–65; innovative approach of, 2; personalizing titles practice at, 26; red rubber ball symbol of, 163–164; sold to Prophet, 42–43

Portfolio clients, 155, 156

"Process Management and Technological Innovation: A Longitudinal Study of the Photography and Paint Industries" study, 137

Prophet: inspiration policy at, 150; Play sold to, 42–43

Purposeful disruption: A.M. Cheers story on, 23; Gerbera daisy bouquet story on, 24–25; ripple effect of, 25; shifting mood through, 21–26

R

Radical Sabbatical: "Rad Sab" mini break form of, 158–159; recharging with a, 157–159

Recognition: A.M. Cheers story on, 23; Gerbera daisy bouquet story on, 24–25

Recombobulation Area, 17

Red Dot international design awards (2006), 52

Red rubber ball symbol (Play), 163–164

Revenue clients, 155–156

Richmond library: Forced Connection of, 114; physical, functional, emotional descriptions of, 102–105; Thief and Doctor process for, 119–120

Richmond Times-Dispatch (newspaper), 42

Rischling, Rich, 153–154

Risk-taking: ask yourself these questions about your, 67; celebrating, 61–63, 65; desperation and, 64–65; using humor as part of, 65–67; producing inspired mindset by, 47, 59–67; worst possible idea to stimulate creativity, 60–61, 108

Rituals: momentum through ideals, symbols, and, 162–166; mood shift through disrupting, 21–22; mood shift through new, 22–25

Roddick, Anita, 31–32

Ross, Ivy, 50–51

S

St. Francis Borgia Church (Wisconsin), 21–22

San Francisco Fairmont, 32

Saturday Night Live (TV show), 108

Saunders, Barry, 36

Scalin, Noah, 88–89

Schrager, Ian, 32

Schweitzer, Peter, 154–155

Sheepwalk idea, 108–109

Silvestri, Tom, 42, 43

Simyone, 135–136

Sixth M: full circle, 167–170

Skull a day story, 88–89

Solutions: accommodating elegant, 98, 99; challenging assumptions by stopping to look for, 84–85; don't overlook the space in between for, 96–98; Dublin college story on, 96–98; Exxon *Valdez* oil spill and hair mat, 5–6

Stefanovich, Jill, 21–22

Stefanovich, Steve, 160

Stop, Start, Continue, 122–124

Storkholm, David, 83

Sturgess, Donna, 42, 136

Sutt, Ed, 111–113

Symbols: momentum through rituals, ideals, and, 162–166; Nationwide's rehabilitated eagles as, 164–165

T

Taking risks. *See* Risk-taking

Tangential inspiration sources: description of, 51–52; examples to compare direct, abstract, and, 54–55

Thief and Doctor, 118–122

Think Cards: focusing on who people are and not what they do, 26; "Go find it" game, 79; idea generation parameters, 97; inspiration for the, 146; living library feature of Swedish public library, 57; measuring behavior, attitudes, innovation, and creativity connections, 137–138; museum mentality, 11–12; one-degree difference, 95; passion and innovative pet food manufacture efficiency, 75; Recombodulation Area, 17; remind yourself that you don't have all the answers, 85; skull a day story on four tenets of creativity, 88–89; there are no absolutes, 83; the three-legged stool, 165; unique places to have a drink, 41

The three-legged stool, 165

3M, 136

Thrift store identity, 39

Timberland, 114–115

Today Show (TV show), 109

Tooke, Lamar, 133

Total Leadership: Be a Better Leader, Have a Richer Life (Friedman), 71

Tower Records, 117

Transformational innovations, 94

Trust, 69, 70

Trustmark, 56–57, 121, 122

Tucker, Kevan, 117

Tushman, Michael, 136–137

U

Unchallenged assumptions, 85–87

The Unidentified (film), 117

University of Pennsylvania, 136

Unwin, John, 32–34

Urban Outfitters, 117

UrbanDaddy (e-mail magazine), 135–136

U.S. Olympic Committee (USOC), 115–118

Use simple language: examples of inserting passion by, 31–33; shifting the mood by, 31–34

V

Velvet Underground, 134

Virginia Community Policing Association, 133

Volvo Your Concept Car (YCC), 48–51

Vosges Haut-Chocolat boutique, 72–73

W

Walacko, Claire, 146

Wald, Abraham, 134–135

Walmart, 86

Walton, Sam, 86

Wardle, Duncan, 38

Washington Square Park, 117

Wellspring program (Good Shepherd Nursing Home), 147

Woolmark Company, 108–109

World War II plane damage story, 134–135

Worst Idea: hooker doll, 60–61, 108; as idea generation mechanism, 107–108; risk-taking to stimulate creativity, 60–61

Y

Yamaguchi, Kristi, 118

Z

Zappos, 132

Zeitgeist curators, 13